For the Love of Teaching

For the Love of TEACHING

And Other Reasons Teachers Do What They Do

Interview Portraits by

IRA D. SHULL

VanderWyk & Burnham
Acton, Massachusetts

Published by VanderWyk & Burnham
A Division of Publicom, Inc.
P.O. Box 2789, Acton, Massachusetts 01720

This book is available for quantity purchases. For information on bulk discounts, call (800) 789-7916 or write to Special Sales at the above address.

Library of Congress Cataloging-in-Publication Data
Shull, Ira D., 1964–

      For the love of teaching : and other reasons teachers do
what they do / interview portraits by Ira D. Shull.

          p.   cm.
      Includes index.
      ISBN 1-889242-03-9

      1. Teachers—United States—Attitudes. 2. Teachers—
United States—Interviews. 3. Teaching—Vocational guidance—
United States. 4. Teacher-student relationships—United States.
I. Title.
LB1775.2.S52   1998
371.1'00973—dc21   97-50058
                                        CIP

Book design by Margaret Ong Tsao

Manufactured in the United States of America
10 9 8 7 6 5 4 3 2 1

For my mother and father

Acknowledgments

Many of the teachers I interviewed for this book welcomed me into their homes or schools. Others met me in restaurants or spent long periods being interviewed on the phone. I am grateful to them as individuals and as a group for their patience, their trust, and their willingness to speak so openly about their lives.

A number of people put me in touch with teachers, including Tanya Auger, Beth DeSombre, Ruth Ann Hayward, Pat Moore, Gene and Angela Parker, Janice Poda, Francesca Pomerantz, Linda Reeder, Carolyn Reeder, Pattie Tobias-Renouard, Lois Safer, Cherie Smith, Barbara Sternlight, and Nancy Wright. Thanks to each of them for their ideas and contributions. Others who contributed to this book in some way are: Kathy Hayden, Stew MacLehose, Bob and Nancy Parker, Bob Reid, Abby Shull, and Hilory Wagner.

Jean Thomas, John FitzGerald, and Pauline Wright gave me valuable feedback about the manuscript with their usual candor and grace. A special thanks to Meredith Rutter and the staff at VanderWyk and Burnham for their encouragement and faith; to Linda Berg and Pam Haley, for their tireless help transcribing interviews; and to John Jacobus, for his wise counsel and friendship.

Linda Rindgen, Dale Griffee, Donald Roberts, Anne Shepherd, Stuart Friebert, Diane Vreuls, Thomas Williams, John Yount, and Frederick Busch are just a few of the great teachers I've had throughout my life. Without them, I would not be the same person.

Finally, I would like to thank my wife, Anne, for her love, support, and editing advice during the most crucial times. I'd also like to thank my parents, Bernard and Janice Shull, for being there. As teachers, as mentors, as friends, their support has never wavered, and their love and respect have never meant so much.

Contents

Foreword

The last twenty-five years have brought new understandings about the nature of intelligence, suggesting that it is not fixed but can be taught. If we take this to be true, it is not too bold a statement to say that qualified teachers hold the fate of our nation in their hands.

This book describes the type of person we need to attract to the teaching profession, as it gives voice to the enthusiasm, the passion, the commitment that invades his or her being. There can be no finer calling, requiring the clearest demonstration of moral and ethical behavior.

Our "best and brightest" will be attracted to teaching far more often when a new management paradigm is implemented. A leading educator, Linda Darling-Hammond writes of the need for learner-centered schools, allowing good teachers to flourish, reducing bureaucratic demands, and favoring competence over procedures. Unfortunately, much of the rhetoric in school reform is directed at structural changes (school-based management), curriculum reform, and the like. Too little attention is given to attracting qualified individuals into the field. We must develop the "teacher as leader"—teachers who clearly see and can seize the opportunities that the growing awareness of the nature of intelligence presents.

While I write this as Chairman of the Center for Arts in the Basic Curriculum, I make my living in the business world. I believe that those of us outside the teaching profession must devote ourselves to creating an environment in our schools where true professionals can thrive. This begins with recognizing that teachers have the capacity to enhance student intelligence, not simply to cover required material.

We must move away from teachers-college graduates who focus almost solely on classroom procedures and methods, and move toward those who have achieved balance in their own abilities through the pursuit of a broadly based academic experience. Qualification in my mind comes with a solid grounding in a particular academic field, as well as a broad, liberal arts background.

Above all, we must expect much more from every student, and find ways to establish a culture of high standards in every school. This is our job, as parents, as working people, and as community members. As we succeed in this mission, it will soon become easier to find qualified young adults willing to devote their lives to teaching to all their students' abilities.

ERIC ODDLEIFSON, JANUARY 1998
Managing Director of GMO Renewable Resources LLC
and Chairman, The Center for Arts in the Basic Curriculum

Author's Preface

The idea for this book began in late 1995 when I was writing a magazine feature article. The nice thing about writing feature articles is that they usually give you a reason to contact people you would never approach otherwise. In this case the article was about teenagers, and how much time they spend "hanging out." I decided that one of the best ways to get inside information—besides going undercover in convenience stores and shopping malls—would be to interview junior high school and high school teachers.

Talking with teachers was nothing new for me. I come from an extended family of them, including both parents, aunts, uncles, and cousins, and I have taught a few courses myself. However, the teachers I began to interview struck me as different. They were all over the country, and they worked with various types of students, including ones considered "learning disabled" and "at risk." For many, connecting emotionally with their students meant more to them than grades, test scores, and even the subjects they were teaching. I began to wonder: what does it mean to be a teacher in this country near the end of the twentieth century, and the millennium?

Over the next two years I interviewed more than fifty teachers throughout the United States. I interviewed at least one teacher in every state, in the District of Columbia, and in Puerto Rico, trying to cover as many different levels, subject areas, and ranges of experience as I could. My goals were modest. I asked them about their lives, and about what made them want to become teachers. I asked them what kept them going, or why they teach. I also asked them to share stories from their teaching experiences. But what I was really asking them for, I realize now, was to share important parts of their lives with me. In return I shared an important part of my life with them.

The edited interviews, which solely reflect the teachers' voices, have been organized into seven thematic sections. When I began, I had a blueprint in my mind for these sections. I thought that all of the teachers' comments would fit into neat categories. I am thankful now that they do not. For these teachers are also individuals, and their comments reflect a wide spectrum of opinion and thought. The themes are not intended to offer definitive reasons about why teachers teach, because I don't think there are definitive reasons. Each teacher has discovered his or her own reason, the way an artist discovers through the process of creating art why it is compelling to do so and what his or her definition of art is.

Near the end of my college years, one of my creative writing teachers asked me to think about my personal aesthetic, or why I write. I had never really considered why I write to be important, because writing came so naturally to me. She urged me to consider it seriously, however, because she said it would help me later in life during the times when I couldn't write, or simply didn't want to. I began working on my aesthetic shortly before graduation. I was twenty-two years old. Twelve years later, I am still figuring it out, and have realized that I will continue to be figuring it out for the rest of my life. The answer is always unfurling ahead of me. When I reach a point where what I've grasped doesn't work any longer, I chase after it some more. I think that's also true of why a lot of the teachers in this book teach.

In a number of ways, compiling these interviews was a return to school for me, but not to any organized class. It was a return to what I remember most fondly about my education: those one-on-one conversations before or after class with teachers in stairwells or hallways, over lunch, or in the quiet sanctity of their offices. In my own experience as a teacher, I have found that important teaching occurs during these exchanges.

All too often in the national discussion about education, teachers are belittled or blamed. I think teachers have a greater influence on all of us than we realize, whether we are children learning to read and write or adults struggling with a new language or culture. By listening to the voices of those who would teach us, we come to understand not only what *learning* means but what *living* means. For it is through our teachers that we begin to discover who we are as human beings, and what we want to be as a society.

I. D. S.
Shirley, Massachusetts
January 1998

For the Love of Teaching

"I live a life and do a job that, if I were independently wealthy, I think I'd be doing anyway."

JOHN ERTEL
Physics Professor
Annapolis, Maryland

Life Work

Many artists consider what they do to be "life work." It is work from which they derive such pleasure and satisfaction that it doesn't seem like work at all. The following teachers feel the same way about teaching. For them, teaching is a kind of compass, an orientation to the world that directs how they see it and how others see them. Teaching is an essential part of who they are and what they experience, in and out of the classroom. For them, the knowledge that teaching is their life work is both invaluable and invigorating.

Kelly Chandler

Kelly Chandler is a graduate instructor in the Education Department at the University of Maine in Orono, where she is also a doctoral student in literacy education. She previously taught English at Noble High School in Berwick, Maine. She has been teaching for six years.

❝ I think it's in my blood to teach. I'm a fourth-generation teacher, and for a long time I thought teaching was the family curse. I wanted to do anything I could to avoid it. I went to Harvard University expecting to be a chemist. But I got a summer job teaching in an enrichment program for teenagers. I realized that there really wasn't anything else that would make me happy.

Being a prospective teacher at Harvard is not an easy thing. You say to people, 'This is what I want to do with my life,' and they say, 'Why didn't you go to the state university and save all that money?' It's a troublesome thing to answer. At the same time, I come from northern Maine, where being a teacher is a way to social respectability. At the University of Maine, you see a lot of first-generation college students who want to be teachers, because along with that degree comes a sense of respect and a place in the community they wouldn't have otherwise.

One of the things that made me angriest about the attitudes I encountered when I said I wanted to be a teacher was that people thought I was too smart. You see a lot of public service commercials on TV talking about how noble it is to be a teacher. And at the same time that teachers are exalted, there's this sense that teachers aren't very smart. People thought I ought to be a doctor or a lawyer or working in business. And I thought, Who needs to be brighter and better prepared than a teacher?

I feel like I'm in the ideal job, whether I'm in a university or in schools working with teachers on-site, or in a high school. It's funny because I've taught, and still teach, with some people who have Foxfire training [an approach to curriculum instruction that builds directly from students' interests and needs]. One of the first things they do is ask kids to describe a shining moment they've had as learners. And I think when you talk about transcendent moments as teachers, it's the same thing coming from the other side. I can think of moments when kids have 'gotten' something right in front of me. There just isn't anything else that feels like that.

The summer after my first year of teaching at Noble, I sent a letter to the kids in my class that said, 'If I run a summer book club, would you come?' There was a pervasive attitude at the school that reading was not a cool thing. But there was this healthy little clan of readers who, once they found out you had a lot of books to lend, would end up in your room after school. I ended up that summer getting seventeen kids.

I chose four contemporary novels that were challenging but were not the kinds of novels they would read in school. I wanted to test how kids would respond to some riskier topics and different kinds of narrative structure. We met every couple of weeks over that summer, on the beach or at somebody's house. We played games and did a lot of social things, which was one of the reasons I think I got seventeen kids. Then we'd spend an hour and a half just sitting around talking about one of the books we'd selected. It was probably one of the most transcendent teaching experiences I've ever had.

I think it gets at something that's true of a lot of teachers I know: teaching is not just something I do. How it goes with a class cuts to the very heart of who I am as a person. I can't leave it in my office and go home and be free of it. And I think that's part of the challenge. There are all kinds of variables you can't control. It doesn't necessarily have to do with how well you prepare. You have to take what you get in front of you every day. 99

Dot Snesrud

Dot Snesrud teaches fifth grade at Osceola Elementary School in Osceola, Nebraska. She has been teaching for twenty-four years.

❝ My fourth-grade teacher is the reason I'm teaching today. I can remember going to lunch my first day in fourth grade. My family had moved from Iowa to Lincoln, Nebraska. I was petrified. The teacher brought me home one afternoon right after lunch. She had a long talk with my folks. From that point on, I was able to adjust better because that teacher took the time for me. I still keep in contact with her.

Osceola is about seventy-five or eighty miles northwest of Lincoln. It's a farming community of nine hundred people. Kindergarten through sixth grade are in one building, and the high school is up the hill. The high-school students walk down to eat lunch in our building. There's a lot of sharing.

The senior class that just graduated this year was exceptional. I remember working my tail off to keep ahead of them when they were fifth graders. For instance, that class decided on its own that it was going to make a time capsule. I suggested each of them write a letter to themselves, knowing it would be opened their senior year. Then I had the capsule sealed and labeled to be reopened in 1997. This year, at the senior picnic, the minute the kids showed up they started saying, 'Do you remember in fifth grade when we did such and such?' When they opened the time capsule, the memories just came pouring out. The letters were amazing because, for one thing, one of our students had fainted on a field trip, and I think every kid but him had that in their letter. The capsule was really a neat experience.

I think a good teacher is one who gives individual time, not just group time—one who sees past grades and papers and realizes there's a person there. In teaching there are days, even years, when that's harder to do. But the teachers I remember are the ones who made you feel important and special as an individual, and who were willing to give that little bit of extra time for things that were important.

Three years ago, I was on loan to the State Department of Education. I lived in Lincoln and ended up house-sitting a couple of blocks from where I grew up. My fourth-grade teacher lived not too far away. One day I called and said, 'Can we get together and visit?' And we did. She dragged me down into her basement. She's been retired for twelve or fifteen years. She had a whole room full of school stuff. Three out of the four kids in my family had had her as a teacher. She actually found a letter my brother had written to her and a picture of my sister.

As we talked, I remembered she was doing things thirty years ago that are being touted today as the way to teach. We actually had a post office, with a postmaster; we all had jobs, and we had to earn money to buy stamps in order to send letters. There was math and writing and socialization. The more we talked, the more I thought she was way ahead of her times. Now we're trying to get back to some of those things.

Teaching isn't as easy as she made it look. But I think there's a difference between an occupation and a vocation. An occupation is a job that you get paid for. A vocation is your life. For me and those teachers who influenced me, teaching is a vocation; it comes so naturally and is so embedded that it's on your mind all the time. **99**

Alvarez Anderson

Alvarez Anderson has taught French and math at high schools in Georgia and South Carolina. He is currently a teacher-in-residence at the South Carolina Center for Teacher Recruitment, a state organization that promotes teaching as a profession within South Carolina. He has been teaching for six years.

❝ I think the fact that I'm a young African-American male has really had an impact on students. I'm a role model for students who probably never get the chance to tell me so, students I may not even teach. I've experienced a lot of things that this generation of students have experienced. I think I'm a little bit more in tune with some of the things going on in their lives. I can understand, and that makes them more apt to open up to me.

I used to teach at a high school in Augusta, Georgia. I taught three classes of *French I*. A *French II* teacher and I would take students to declamation contests where they would memorize poetry, recite it, and get awards. There was an African-American male who was in the *French II* class. I helped him with his pronunciation once but never really got to have any other contact with him. I only knew his name from riding on the bus to the competitions. I left that school, came home to South Carolina, and on occasion went back to Augusta. One time I stopped by the school. I was standing there talking to the *French II* teacher, and this guy came down the hall. I spoke to him. He said, 'I'm not talking to you.' I tried but couldn't figure out what I'd done, so I asked, and he said, 'Well, you just left. Now I don't have anybody to look up to when I come to school.' It sounds simple, but I thought about that for a long time. He was watching me to see what I was doing, how I was carrying myself, what I stood up for. I think teachers need to understand that their jobs extend far beyond the classroom. Everything we do is a part of our teaching.

I went through college with the idea that I wanted to be a lawyer. I took education courses because it was considered something to fall back on. I've since learned that was the wrong reason; teaching's not a profession you need to settle for. I went to law school for a year and it turned out it was totally different from my personality, totally different from what I needed to be doing. When I talk to students, I never knock any profession they want to do. But it has to be something you internally desire. Deep in my heart, there's some reason I'm a teacher. I think that I'm *supposed* to be.

A lot of teachers develop a negative viewpoint about the profession because we're usually at the bottom of the decision-making pole. We have to start emphasizing the positives ourselves. Then other people out there who are not teachers will see it as a more respectable profession. I think that's very important.

You have to understand where you teach, the students you teach, the teachers you teach with, and see if your personality fits with all of them. You really have to investigate and make sure teaching is what you want. You need to have that drive, and that compassion. 99

Dolly Winger

Dolly Winger teaches grades seven through twelve English at North Sargent High School in Gwinner, North Dakota. She has also taught theater and psychology. She has been teaching for twenty-eight years.

66 Some of my first memories are of playing school upstairs in my parents' farmhouse. My mom was a Sunday-school teacher, so she had lots of flannel board, which is cardboard covered with flannel. She had flannel graph paper that had a kind of early Velcro on the back, which would stick to the board; this was a way a teacher could do a presentation. So I would sneak my mom's flannel board out of her Sunday-school materials and use it to give my bears and dolls a reading lesson. Of course, I always had to be the teacher; it was too hard to pretend to be the pupil.

Eastern North Dakota is entirely flat. It's prairie. The thing that distinguishes Gwinner is that it's the home of the Bobcat, the front-end loader. This is where we make them and ship them out by the truckload all over the world. There are six hundred people in this town. A thousand people work at the factory, so they come from many little towns to work here. Like other North Dakota towns, we struggle to survive, and to keep the school enrollment up. It's generally thought that if the school folds, the community folds. A great part of me loves living here because the air is perfectly clean. We're essentially without crime. To me, those things are very valuable.

I'm a one-person department; I have all the students in the school. That's not that unusual in North Dakota. I typically go to school at 7:00 A.M. I never come home before 7:00 P.M., and it's more typical that I come home at 10:00 P.M. I've been known to come home at midnight, and one time last year I stayed all night. I feel bad that I don't want to go home, that it's 8:00 at night and I'm just having so much fun doing my stuff at school. Sometimes when I'm home I want to go back to school because it seems like great fun. It can get very laborious, but putting the lessons together, rearranging the room, and thinking of new ideas are fun. I'm enrolled in a summer master's program, and the first thing the dean said in week one was, 'I hope that none of you are the kind of people who are letting your jobs consume you.' But my job does consume me. And I love it!

Being a teacher can be a great benefit if you're a creative person. Somebody once said a good test is to go into an empty room and sit for an hour without the benefit of any stimulation—if you can be happy for that hour, then perhaps you can be a teacher. I agree.

The work in your life should be something that's going to be of significant value to the human race. I know that sounds crazy because somebody has to put peaches in the peach cans; I might need a can of peaches one day. But I want to touch somebody's life. I think that teachers do touch lives. It's a high and lofty goal. I care about my kids. I want them to fly away, to go learn something else about the rest of the world.

I have a friend in Montana who's a magnificent teacher. He affects people, but he's not satisfied with affecting some—he wants to affect them all. I've always wanted to say to him, 'You're not God. That was God's goal, and he hasn't been successful. How can you want that in the classroom?' But I think maybe it's what I want, too. 99

Judy Adair

Judy Adair is a resource specialist for academically gifted children at Westwood Elementary School in Broken Arrow, Oklahoma. She has been teaching for twenty-three years.

❝ I try to teach kids the same way that I learn. If it's simply that they've never seen an earthworm before, then isn't it time to really look at one? To me, learning is discovery, and that leads to more learning. It's a lifetime process. I'm still doing it three years away from retirement. I'm still thinking, What can I do this year? and Isn't this great? and Look how this works—isn't it wonderful? That enthusiasm just pours over to the kids.

So much teaching goes on outside of classrooms. As educators, if we don't somehow tie into that, then we're missing a lot. There's a learning opportunity everywhere; children need to see that so they can recognize it in their own lives. I'm big on nature walks outside the school building. We'll write things on the board that we're going to look for that day. Once we found an owl pellet. We didn't expect to; I had no idea that owls lived on top of our building. I've had kids say to me, 'You know, I've been out here many times on my bike and I've never seen this.' That's it, isn't it? It's the stopping and looking at something. I'll tell kids that if you look at something closely enough, you'll learn about it.

At any age in your life there's some boundary you haven't crossed, and if you're open, there's always a new horizon. That's a wonderful thing. I try to instill that in children and to keep their spark alive; they have a special ability to learn faster and deeper, and we should just go with it. I've learned so much myself through teaching. I once had a group of kids who wanted to do photography. We built a darkroom and did it. I try to let the kids see me as a human being, with all my fallibility. I let them know that I've never done something before, and if we fall flat on our faces, we'll just get up and go on. I didn't know if we could build a darkroom or develop a picture, but I said let's go try. The creative process—taking an idea from an abstract concept in my mind to reality—is probably one of the things that gives me the greatest joy in life.

I believe what keeps me going is the exploration of learning. Maybe it's a simple thing—maybe the children have never seen a butterfly emerge from a pupa. Or, you ask them to create a poem or share some feeling that in some way reveals who they are to everybody in the room—that's taking a chance as big as trying to jump over the Grand Canyon on a motorcycle. Being able to do that is what life's about.

I don't think I'll ever stop being a teacher. I have a lot of teacher friends, and we're teaching each other all the time. 'Come look at this,' we'll say, or 'You ought to go do this.' If you truly want to be a teacher, it's in your heart to share what you find out and what you know. There's nothing like it for connecting with people. What other occupation has the opportunity to touch someone's life in a way that's positive and can last forever? Not many people can do that in their jobs. 🙶

Dave Swanson

Dave Swanson teaches English, drama, speech, and reading at Greenfield Community High School in Greenfield, Iowa. He has been teaching there for twenty-five years.

66 I can't come up with one, single reason why I teach. I enjoy the contact with the kids; that's one thing. Is it to repay a debt, a societal debt? I was basically educated in Iowa. I'm not living in the same community, but I have a responsibility in my own mind to repay the people who gave me the tools to meet the world head on. I've always told myself that if there were four days in a row when I really had to get jump-started to go to school in the morning, I'd get out of education. I've never had that happen. I like to get up in the morning; I look forward to it. If I weren't in a formal classroom, people would still think I'm a teacher. They tell me that. I've been a gun dealer for about fifteen years, and when I do gun shows on weekends, they say, 'You explained that really well.' If I ever got over being shy, I could be a salesman.

Greenfield is a county seat town of 2200 people. We have shared programs with all of the little schools around here. The county only has 8000 people. Everybody is involved in one way or another in agriculture. The merchants are dependent upon whether we get rain and if we have good corn prices. We have an average of 55 kids to a grade at the upper levels. They've grown up in a pocket of America that could have come right out of the 1930s, out of something Steinbeck wrote. There's no Hardee's or McDonald's. The school supplies maybe 50 percent of the community's activities. The older people in this town walk every day, from 5:00 in the morning until 6:30, and then a lot of times also from 7:30 in the evening until maybe 10:00. Kids who have in-line skates will skate down the street. We don't have a stoplight in this town. It's a little different; life is a little slower here.

For the most part, the people I teach with are the same ones I've been teaching with for over ten years. Some of them I've taught with for twenty-five years. We all have a similar outlook: teaching's just part of us. All of us need the money; we have house and car payments to make like anyone else. But I really think—and I'm speaking for more than just myself—that we would be teachers even if we weren't getting paid what we are. There are a lot of things that are as satisfying and as valuable as money, like being happy with yourself and making a positive and lasting contribution to your community. In four or five years, the kids I teach are going to have children of their own. I'm not trying to say I instill values. It goes beyond just showing or introducing them.

I've gone through the grief of losing a student to a traffic accident. To this day, on Fridays, I tell my students, 'Be careful, don't drink and drive, don't ride with people that do, wear your seatbelt, have a good weekend, I'll see you on Monday.' I don't know if that impacts anybody, except that every kid I have on Friday knows they're going to hear that, and when I don't tell them, somebody's always going,

'Swan, Swan, do your speech!' If it keeps one kid from getting in the car with a bunch of people who have been drinking, it's time well spent.

I really view my subject area as life. The sign on my door says *Reading for Life and Pleasure.* The values I introduce will last a long time after I'm gone. And I plan on living to 120!🙨🙨

Suzanne Caldwell

Suzanne Caldwell teaches Spanish and chairs the Language Department at Central High School in Little Rock, Arkansas. She has been teaching for seventeen years.

❝ I try to bond with the kids. I'm not that warm a person, but I do seem to be able to connect with them. They know I'm doing the best I can to help them learn. I serve as a coach. So many of them have an attitude that it's them against the teacher, that they've got to trick me out of their grade or fight me in some way. We have to go through an initial period when I prove to them that I'm on their side. I'm not one of the team, but I am there to help them. Whatever I do for them is going to be for the best.

Central High School is four stories high and two blocks long. There were well-known desegregation clashes at the school in 1957, so we have quite a history. It's right in the middle of gang territory. We have about eight security guards. We have searches with metal detectors; we have drug dogs that sometimes come through the halls. It's just a way of life for us. We don't think anything about it.

One thing I like about teaching is being able to control my environment. I can create a positive atmosphere every day, one that I enjoy and that I feel kids can learn in. I tell them that I don't know everything. That's hard because sometimes they say, 'Oh, you don't know that?' They think they've won a victory because other teachers have perhaps tried to tell them that they know everything. There's no way to know everything in a foreign language. One reason I stay with it is because there's always something else to learn.

I also feel I'm raising the kids that come into my classroom. They say, 'I spend more time with you than I spend with my parents.' That puts me in a very influential position. You've got to appreciate and respect them as people. An example of that is my youngest daughter (who is going to be a Spanish teacher as well but presently teaches preschool). She had me drive up to Fayetteville, which is three hours away, to meet her students, who are between two and a half and three years old. She's already seeing them as separate individuals. I think that's important.

I think that whenever you do something major in your life—and teaching is major in mine—it's not only a job, it's like a mission. Everything I do is centered around my profession. Whatever I'm doing, I'm learning. With Spanish, I get to grow. The levels I teach don't have a set curriculum, so every year I get to decide what I'm going to do. The kids will say, 'Don't you get bored teaching the same thing?' I tell them that I never teach the same thing. I size up the class; I see what they need; I figure out how I'm going to meet the need.

I'm not a performer type of person, but if I'm tired or have been up too late, the kids give me the energy to keep going. I have an opportunity to have input into a lot of lives, and I get a lot back.

Sally Gibson

Sally Gibson is an elementary art specialist at Pike Lake Elementary School in New Brighton, Minnesota. She has been teaching for twenty-eight years.

❝ When I judge a child's work of art, I never judge it on the production element. If we're teaching warm and cool colors that week, and they can explain to me, 'I painted the sky red and the trees yellow because I want a warm feeling,' well, that's valid. I really don't look at it in terms of what's good or bad. I think that helps the children feel better about what they're doing, knowing that I'm going to be accepting of whatever they're creating.

So much of the world is visual. I want them to take all the pieces into account, not just fine art. In third grade we play a game called What Is Art? We put a big circle on the table. I give them all these images [pictures I have found in various sources], and they pretend the images are the real thing. I say, 'This is a horse you're looking at' or 'This is a famous Rembrandt.' Then I say, 'Now put inside the circle what you think is art, and outside the circle that which isn't art. If you're not sure, put it on the line.' It's really interesting to listen to the kids debate this. Then I help them generate some parameters for what art is. We might come up with the statement that art expresses an idea or a feeling, or that art is made by people. An elephant walking across paper may be pleasing, but [the elephant] didn't purposely manipulate those elements. It was an accident. Then they go back and regroup their images. So when they leave third grade, they've got a pretty good understanding of what art is and how very much of their world is art.

I like what I do. I can't think of a better job. I think if you go back in time, you find that art is really the way people have communicated with one another to express everything from spirituality to politics. I don't know how we would get along without it.

I like kids, but that's not the reason I'm in teaching. What I've got to share, I think, is important in their lives. I'm a much better teacher now than I was twenty-eight years ago. In art especially, you get so many variations, or ways of seeing. At the end of the day, I probably go home wiser from what I've picked up from my students. I think to teach is to live, to see this future generation coming through your classroom and to have an impact on it. I just really like the feeling. There are some days I go home and say, 'Why am I doing this?' But then there's something on TV that triggers something we could do in class. Or I go through a museum and get excited. I get these wonderful student teachers who give me ideas and things to work with.

I feel really alive when I'm in my classroom. I'm one of those people who look forward to fall because I've spent all summer amassing things that got me excited and that might get the children excited. A student just brought in a book of Gary Larson cartoons. It's called *Wiener Dog Art*. There was a joke in there on Labrador Dolly. They got such a kick out of it.

When I was little, my dad instilled in me that if all of us leave our own corner of the world a little bit better than when we found it, society will persevere. I think I do that with my kids. Besides just teaching art, I touch on the environment, and morality in a very small way—what the kids believe to be right or wrong. I think in this arena, in the art room, the ideas are really respected. Kids go away feeling a little more self-confident.

They're very proud of their artwork. I try to get it all matted and displayed around the school. I've gotten part of it into an art exhibit that tours the United States. I send out the artwork in the fall and it comes back in the spring. The exhibit goes to eight different schools. I put their artwork on display in shopping centers. I have a big art show in the spring, and the kids will walk through and say, 'I did that,' and they'll talk about how it relates to symmetry. The third graders just did some pottery that focused on how artists use symmetry in their compositions. The words they use are just so literate. It's almost like gardening—you plant these seeds, and if you add the right stuff, they might just grow up and be what you hoped for. 🙶

John Ertel

John Ertel is an associate professor of physics at the United States Naval Academy in Annapolis, Maryland. He also served as a pilot in the Marine Corps. He has been teaching for twenty-seven years.

66 I never really knew I was interested in teaching. My mother was an operating room supervisor, and I grew up in a hospital. Most people expected me to be a physician. I was also heavily involved in the Boy Scouts. As an Eagle Scout, I used to take great delight in teaching the other kids skills. I didn't really think then that I was a teacher. When I went into the Marine Corps, I spent a lot of my time teaching in survival schools. When I was overseas, looking at coming back to the States, they asked me what I'd like to do. I said I'd be happy to be a flight instructor. Again, the word *teacher* never came up. It's amazing that you can get so far into something and never realize what you're doing.

The rewards I find in teaching are the same ones I got when I was a Boy Scout teaching other kids how to light fires, weave rope, and handle themselves with a map and compass. For some reason, people like me derive a great deal of pleasure from watching people learn; I have no idea why. I do know that when you see students for whom it isn't happening, it's downright painful to watch. I know some students could do the work even if I was never there—if we just brought them in, gave them the book, and told them, 'Here's the stuff you need to learn'—there's a certain amount of pleasure in watching them do it on their own. And for that broad spectrum in between who aren't going to fall by the wayside but also aren't going to get it on their own without your help, I don't know why there's so much enjoyment. Somehow, I think I was just meant to be a teacher. Knowing that you played a critical role in giving this large midground of students the tools for most of the successes in their lives is the principal reward.

My students go through a remarkable amount of hell. They have a schedule that would just kill most people. I don't believe I could have survived it as a student. Some of my best students have fallen asleep in class. They don't fall asleep because they're bored; it's that they're so tired and their schedule is so heavy. I have a great deal of respect for any young person who can come here as a midshipman and live in the regimented style they do, under the schedule they have. I'm amazed that so many of them seem to be able to do it.

A lot of people think of a typical military person as very work-oriented but somewhat narrow in his or her thought processes. I've not found that to be true. The breadth of the midshipmen's interests is, again, just amazing to me. A number of them are out there in the public schools doing Mids for Kids, a reading intervention program for students who are at risk educationally. They're also involved in Habitat for Humanity, helping to build or rehab homes for people who would never be able to own a home otherwise. They spend a lot of time they don't have doing remarkable good turns.

There's a great deal of pleasure derived from graduation day, when you see people walk across the stage and you know they can handle anything life throws at them. You look at the reward on the faces of their parents and other friends and relatives, and you know you've had some part in that. I'm constantly amazed that people let me do it and I don't have to pay them. When I don't teach, or I'm away from it for too long, I miss it. My wife, who also used to teach here, puts it this way: 'If you have to ask why teaching is enjoyable, we'll never be able to tell you.'

I was talking to someone from my high school graduating class the other day. She was really just bowled over that I had not become a physician. She said, 'You never went to medical school?' I said no. Then she asked, 'Are you happy?' I said, 'I live a life and do a job that, if I were independently wealthy, I think I'd be doing anyway. So I think I must be pretty darn happy.' 99

"I have significant relationships that matter."

JUDY MOORE ENO
Montessori Classroom Guide
San Antonio, Texas

Connection

There is a simple, uncluttered joy most people feel when they connect emotionally or spiritually with others. For the following teachers, personal connection helps to explain why they teach. Some of these teachers are part of school communities where they feel accepted; for others, connection happens on a smaller scale and outside of traditional classrooms. Connection means sharing parts of themselves with students, not only as teachers but as people. It is about building relationships over a period of time and sustaining them. For these teachers, personal connection is what makes them thrive.

Peter Walter

Peter Walter teaches reading at the Linden Hill School, a private school for dyslexic adolescent boys in Northfield, Massachusetts. Born with a learning disability himself, he overcame its problems through a course of hard work and discipline that included military school, athletics, and self-determination. He has lived and taught on and off at Linden Hill School for twenty-nine years.

66 For me, there are three different attitudes we can have in life. We can be deadly serious, wildly enthusiastic, or we can have a sense of humor. All I want to give my kids is a sense of humor, and at their level. Jokes are monumental for them. They have never been able to read. And what's one of the first things kids read? A book of riddles. My kids never knew any riddles. Riddles were perplexing and agonizing for them. So I deal a lot with puns, with a playful use of language, because I want them to be able to laugh and enjoy language and ideas.

We had a boy who wouldn't talk when he came here. I pointed at my foot and said, 'What's this?' He said, 'A shoe,' and I said, 'God bless you.' He said, 'May I call my mother?' He got on the phone and said, 'What do you have on your foot?' and his mother said, 'A shoe,' and he said, 'God bless you.' He turned to me and he said, 'You got any more?' And he taught me. He taught me that the reason kids say 'I don't care' is that they have nothing to share.

All I want for them is cognizance. I want them to look at life and live it and experience it and feel it and think it and know it. I want them to know what they think, know what they feel, and know what they know. I want those three things to be very clear—I think, I feel, I know—because when somebody asks you a question, you've got to know whether you're saying what you think, what you feel, or what you know. People frequently say what they feel or think and make it appear it's what they know. But they don't know. And that's why Socrates said, 'I know that I do not know. And therefore I am smarter than those who think they know but do not know.' And when I teach, I always keep that in mind.

At one point, I was unemployed for seven years. I went to Tennessee, and I *stopped*. I went into the woods and I looked, I read, I sat down. It took me two years to stop—two years before I had nothing to do, no reason to get up, no restlessness, no impulsiveness. I lament not having a wife, not having children, my own home, but I never lament those seven years when I actually stopped. For five of them, I *lived*. One man in the community said that I should be given a stipend for the rest of my life. He said, 'We should let you come here and live,' because every day I went out and talked to people, I went out and enjoyed life and shared it with others. I ran a lot, but I also played soccer and told stories to children. I took people on picnics and took them caving. Everybody knew me—everybody. I had dogs, and I'd take them for walks in the morning, and runs, and one morning I had twelve dogs with me. I also used to run with horses. I had a horse there, actually, that ran next to me without a rider. So I'd go with this horse, and a dog, and the three of us would run through the woods. Those were my happiest moments. Running was so primitive for me. I loved to be primitive, to be simple. I got joy from just putting one foot in front of the other.

I think what I've experienced in life is very much like the cave analogy in Plato. I got up, and I saw that there was a light, and I was determined to go back and explain it to other people even if they resisted. And that's just what Plato said would happen when you try to show them a light—they're going to fight you, they're not going to want to see it. Sometimes I'm not as tolerant as other people think I might be, and Plato said that also happens to you, because you've seen the light and you don't do very well in the dark. That's why I teach. I know what the boys are going through, not absolutely, but I have a good idea because I went through it myself.

We had a boy who came here years ago and died of cancer at twenty-one. When he died, I wrote a poem. It's called 'Sand Castle' and it goes, 'I took so much pride/and now he has died./Make another,/make another./Why?/All will be washed away./But, oh, how he could play/and he always had something to say./It was he/who was perfect pay.' Just working with him was worth every bit of my life. And when he died, it was like watching a sand castle get washed away. When he came here, he was a bed wetter, he swore like a trooper, he caused more trouble than you could ever possibly imagine. And yet within him was a core of life, and you knew that when all that other stuff faded away, he was going to be one phenomenally beautiful person. And he made it.

Life is all attitudinal. It comes down to deciding, 'Are you gonna get up and go . . . ?' And that's what I try to do in my classroom. I project energy; I project enthusiasm; I project life. I'm an artist and my canvas is my class. What I produce depends on those boys, and my interaction with them. And just like every artist, I make every stroke count. Every little line is important for me, and every stroke, and every aspect of what I'm doing with them.99

Tim Lang

Tim Lang has taught English at School One, an independent high school in Providence, Rhode Island. Recently, he began teaching at Ben Franklin International School in Barcelona, Spain. He has been teaching for four years.

❝❝ My introduction to teaching was through volunteer work, or stipend work, which is basically volunteer work with another name—the pay is like pizza money. So a lot of times it's amazing to me that teaching is work. It doesn't feel like it. I don't put on a suit every day. I'm with other people and talking about ideas; I'm helping people, interacting with them, and trying to do positive things. It's a great job.

School One is for kids who have not been successful in traditional high schools. What they're really looking for and what we try to give them is an environment where they're respected and treated as adults. They choose their own classes within a certain framework of requirements, like a university. I also run a service-learning class. My students and I go to a local elementary school that has predominantly English as a Second Language students, and we work with young kids in classrooms a couple of hours a week. For my kids it's fabulous. They get to be mentors; they get a sense of being in charge of something. Most kids, unfortunately, haven't really been given that chance. We have kids who are eighteen and nineteen years old. I'm twenty-five, so we're not talking about a huge age difference. Yet, there is room for some real growth.

We have kids who we know are substance abusers. I'm originally from New Orleans, and between my junior and senior years of college, I interned in the district attorney's office. Teenagers would walk in and get thrown in jail. Who knows what happened to them? You're sixteen or seventeen years old, the cop pulls you over and finds a bag of marijuana in your glove compartment, and two weeks later you're in jail. There's not much room for growth there.

When you're working with kids day in and day out and talking with them in a realistic way, hopefully that makes a difference. I've seen kids who have come out of rehab, serious users, and really turned things around. I think that within that framework, being a teacher can be a very political act. The breadth you have in communicating skills and values to kids who aren't going to find them in other places is awesome and surprising.

Being the adviser of a student who grew up in an alcoholic household, and having that student's trust and confidence—having that student value my opinion—is a huge responsibility. It's one I take very seriously. Whether I were teaching or doing something else, it would be about making connections with people and finding ways to make a positive difference in the world—in my own little corner of it. I go in plenty of days and teach bad classes, but the kids are there the next day, and I'm there the next day, and we go at it again. When I'm there they know it, and that's important. I treat them in a way that's human. Do I think I'm making a difference? I wouldn't be doing it if I weren't.

Penny Cruz

Penny Cruz teaches grades seven through twelve music at the University School of Milwaukee, an independent school in Milwaukee, Wisconsin. She has also taught music to children in kindergarten through eighth grade. She is Asian-American and has been teaching for seven years.

❝❝ I got interested in teaching because of music. I really wanted to conduct, and a lot of the people I saw who were models for conducting were teachers. In high school I was given the opportunity to help coach young string quartets and the oboe section in a community orchestra. Those experiences made me see what I could do, and that's the kind of thing I'm doing now.

I grew up and went to school in an almost totally white community, so the assimilation is pretty strong. I'll get comments from people who say, 'I always forget you're not white.' People who think of Asians tend to think of people who look more Chinese or Japanese. My last name is Hispanic, and in the places where I've taught, some people have thought I'm Latino; others have thought black or Indian. It's very interesting how people approach my ethnicity. It wasn't until maybe two months before school let out this past year—I'm a new teacher—that a couple of kids asked me about it. 'We've been speculating,' they said. 'We didn't know.'

It follows through my life, not just my teaching. When I left to go to college, one of the issues I was facing was not wanting to be in a community like the one I grew up in. Then I found myself in the same sort of situation in both of my teaching experiences. In University School, there are only three of us who are not white, two African-Americans and myself. And there are maybe a hundred teachers.

I recently went to a meeting of SEED [Seeking Education Equality and Diversity]. It's a book group made up of teachers, administrators, and parents in the community that discusses readings on multicultural issues. I walk in, and I always feel like, 'Well, speaking for my people, and people of color everywhere . . . ,' which I think is an unfair situation to be in. But I know there are Asian students who are facing the same issues, who live in the same way that I did when I was in high school. So University School is an important place for me to be.

I've been talking with other music teachers about how it seems there are so many people out there who want some sort of connection with other people. Music is where I've made my strongest connection—with other people, with aesthetics, with myself. As a singer, I'm always involved with a text—with words, with speaking or getting something across through the music—and it's that expressivity I find so valuable in my day-to-day life. In some ways I'm a very expressive person and in some ways I'm not. Music has always been an outlet for my expressivity.

When I see students experiencing the kind of emotion, the kind of commitment to text that's required of a singer, I find it really exciting. The kids who come into chorus, especially in high school, come because their friends are in it, or they like the teacher or they know that they're pretty good singers and want to perform. My job is to make it so that they can't imagine their day without music. My greatest success will not be what happens in my classroom, but when my students continue to sing and continue to need music in their lives once they leave me.

That's what I want to carry to them. All sorts of connections have been made for me through music. 99

Kathy France

Kathy France is program coordinator for the Youth Teaching Youth Program at the Utah Museum of Natural History in Salt Lake City, Utah. The program trains seventh and eighth graders to teach beginning science to elementary-school students throughout the city. She has been teaching for eleven years.

66 The personal growth within these kids has been phenomenal. Watching them grow physically is pretty amazing, too. I didn't think they could grow that fast. Three of them are looking down at me, and last year at this time I was looking down at them.

They've all developed their own teaching styles. I'll take four of my kids out to teach a class of thirty. The students break into groups of five or six, second through fourth graders. One of my kids is smaller than all the fourth graders he's ever taught, yet he's never had an ounce of trouble. He has a manner about him that keeps the students organized and focused. Another of my kids is a real authoritarian. He's Hispanic, and he's really funny. He claims not to speak Spanish, but at a lot of the schools we go to, English is a second or a third language. He comes over and tells me in English what a kid just said in Spanish. He'll just tell me flat out what's going on over there. He pulls the Dad thing on them.

Then there's the kid from El Salvador. He's got to be one of the ten smartest kids I've ever encountered. When we go to a school that has Spanish-speaking students, I take him along, and he'll teach his entire lesson in Spanish. If he has English speakers in the group, he'll turn around and do it double time in English. It's just amazing. He's bright. He's cute. He's always telling me, 'I'm Latin. Women love me!' I'm, like, 'You've got to get a grip, honey.' Sometimes, I've never felt as old as after I've spent eight hours with him.

The thing that gets me going in the morning is the kids. They're a riot; they're fun. You can put a twist on anything and make them think they're having a great time. In the end, they do have a good time. Part of what keeps me going, too, is the fact that I love science, and I hate the fact that very few other people do. It seems that they like it at this stage of the game, but they hate it in ninth grade. So if I can just keep them going, convince them long enough and hard enough that after ninth grade it's still going to be fun, then I've done something.

The effects of this program are long-range. We've had two boys end up on the state honor roll. Another boy went to the finals of the state history fair. These are kids who have been capable but, according to their parents, never showed this kind of interest.

Just knowing that I've had a good impact on a kid is what makes it worthwhile. There are kids I taught in Montana six years ago whom I'm still in contact with. So many people have poor impacts on kids. I saw something that said it takes twenty-two adults to raise a child from infancy to adulthood. I like being one of those twenty-two. It's an important role. It's very important that kids have role models outside of their parents. They need to see that there are other adults out there they can emulate. Middle school seems to be the age when they start to think Mom and Dad suck. If that's the case, you want to be the adult who doesn't. ❞

Teri Holler

Teri Holler has taught reading, language arts, history, math, science, and speech at grades seven through twelve. She lives in Troy, Alabama. She has been teaching for nineteen years.

I've known people who have tried teaching and left after one semester, saying, 'No, I don't want to do this.' I think what keeps you wanting to teach is the excitement and joy you feel when you do find a student or two or four whom you really connect with. You feel like you're moving their lives toward what they're going to do as adults. You can get a lot of satisfaction out of that.

At one point, I was going through some personal difficulties. I was having a rough time in the classroom, and it surprised me how understanding some of my junior high students were. I was spending a lot of time on things like being a student council sponsor in addition to my regular teaching. They seemed to realize that I was having problems, and they appreciated the fact that I was helping them. Often you get a lot back from the kids who participate in those kinds of things. You don't get as much back from unmotivated kids. But every once in a while, you'll touch them somehow, and all of a sudden there's positive feedback coming from them, too.

I used to teach in an alternative school in Odessa, Texas. It was a school for students who'd been expelled from the school district for weapons, alcohol, or drugs. It was a really aggravating experience; it got to the point where I felt I was in danger of physical harm. But I also had a young man who wound up there because he'd been involved with the wrong group; he shouldn't have been there. I made some strides with him. He was Hispanic and had a lot of difficulty reading because of his difficulty with English. He lived with his parents and his grandparents, and none of them spoke English. School was the only place where he had to deal with it. He had some learning difficulties, too, and had moved into that district from elsewhere after starting school in Mexico. I don't think any teacher anywhere along the line had spent much time working with him one-on-one. One thing about that alternative school was that you could spend considerable time working one-on-one with a student.

I worked with him quite a bit and was seeing some improvement. His reading and comprehension were getting better, and he was actually choosing to read when he had free time, which he'd never have done before. Then his court date came up and he was sent off to juvenile detention. I don't know what happened to him; I wish there was a way to know. The Texas prisons have their own school system, so I hope there was someone where he went who continued to work with him. This was a young person who could be helped with some attention, some time, and some effort. It's wonderful when you find one of these students and you can do something for them.

Susan Thurman

Susan Thurman teaches English at Henderson County High School in Henderson, Kentucky. She has also taught English at the junior-high level. She has been teaching for twenty-six years.

❝ I hate the first part of the semester, when I don't have any history with my students. I can't say, 'What did you do yesterday?' or 'What were you telling me about?' until I get to know them. Today a student told me a story about locking her keys in her car. A firetruck had to come, and then another firetruck, and it was just this long thing. Some of the students come to me with problems, or tell me about their dates over the weekend. They keep me interested in teaching. Plus I like learning, and I hope I give them some kind of spark about that. Every day when I teach—I guess it's part of becoming older—I realize how much I don't know.

Some students just want to get through class; they just want to get that credit. I always think back to my geology class in college. I was mildly interested in geology, but I didn't want to major in it. That's the way a lot of kids are about some of the subjects they aren't taking as electives. They aren't going to be the stars of the class, but they're going to be fine people. I teach the children of some of my former students, who have turned out to be productive, with good jobs, and happy. Just because they weren't interested in English, or whatever I was teaching at the time, doesn't reflect badly on them. We don't know what was going on in their lives that caused them not to study, or just not to be interested.

I saw this girl in the grocery a year or so ago. She's maybe in her thirties now, and she said, 'I had you when I was in junior high. What I remember most is that one time I got the highest grade in the class, and you let me sneak into the teacher's room and call my mother and tell her.' I don't remember that! I would never have thought this would be the highlight of that girl's junior-high career. It's just that sort of thing; you never know what kind of mark you're making on kids. You never know what they're going to pick up on. It's made me think every once in a while: What am I going to do today that somebody's going to remember more than what a vocabulary word means— what act of kindness that has nothing to do with what we're studying?

Under Kentucky law I can retire next year after twenty-seven years. People have started asking me if I'm going to. I don't think I will. I just enjoy it too much. The paperwork gets me down, and sometimes the politics. But when you can get in that room and close the door and teach, and just see some folks smile, that's nice. 99

Colette Lenfest

Colette Lenfest has taught college-level Spanish at the University of Illinois at Urbana-Champaign, Ohio University, and Bridgewater State College in Bridgewater, Massachusetts. She has also taught English as a Second Language (ESL) to Polish immigrants in a community-based setting in Chicago. She has been teaching for five years.

66 You really feel like you achieve something when you're teaching. You start off at the beginning of a semester and everyone is sort of inhibited, not wanting to even say *hola,* or 'hello,' in Spanish. By the end you have them giving presentations and you can really see their progress. They say things like, 'I'm going to take Spanish next semester.' It's such a gratification to feel like you've shared something with someone.

Every student, especially a beginning student, has a fear of learning. When you're signing up for physics and you've never taken a science course before, there's a fear of, What am I getting into? I recently had the same feeling. I'd been wanting to take art classes for years. I hadn't taken one since grammar school. I signed up for a painting class, and I thought, I wonder if I should drop this—I don't have any talent, so what am I doing? I was terrified before the first day of class. I can imagine that some of my students feel the same thing. You see them the first day and they don't want to say anything. Those are the students who often start coming out of their shells by the middle of the semester. You don't have to call on them anymore; they'll raise their hands, or they'll come up to you after class. To me, that's great. To help someone overcome that fear is great.

I used to go to restaurants with my Polish students. A lot of times they would want me to take the initiative to order. Several months later, they wanted to order for themselves. I felt the same thing in my painting class with my professor. It took me an hour before I could even put a dot of paint on the canvas. By the end, I was painting someone's portrait, and I was happy that I was able to do it. Once you help people overcome that fear, they can go on themselves.

There's even a certain fear involved in teaching. I know that before every semester, I've always been incredibly nervous, even though I taught three classes the previous semester and did a fine job. People can give you advice, but you really learn to teach when you're in a classroom. It's kind of hard to prepare otherwise. You become a teacher when you step inside and feel how you work with people.

Part of the challenge is discovering new ways to teach. My father is a good example. He's always been a traditional language teacher using a textbook, and in the past five or ten years he's really gotten creative. I can see a complete change in his attitude. He's having a wonderful time teaching. He's incorporating soap operas into his teaching of foreign languages. You have to try different things as a teacher. You have to adopt a style, but never be afraid to experiment, just as your students are experimenting by taking your class. 🙶🙶

Judy Moore Eno

Judy Moore Eno is the middle-school coordinator and a classroom guide at the Judson Montessori School in San Antonio, Texas. She began teaching in an urban public high school, and has also taught English as a Second Language (ESL) and adult basic education. She has been teaching for twenty-four years.

❝ I come from a long line of teachers. I didn't know this until about eight years ago. My father was an Air Force pilot, so I grew up on military bases in Japan, California, Ohio, Alabama, and Virginia, even though my family is from Texas. I started doing genealogy and discovered teachers on both sides of the family. My brother calls me his first teacher, so if you count that, I guess I started when I was thirteen months old.

The Montessori classroom is not teacher-centered. That's the really dramatic difference from the teaching I did in public school. The environment is carefully prepared. Classroom teachers are called *guides,* because their job is to guide students. I'm trying to create an environment that calls to the students. My most important work is deciding what to put in and what to leave out.

Maria Montessori [the founder of Montessori education] wrote that children at the middle-school level need to farm. She recommended that they be responsible, with adult supervision, for making the whole farm work. What she says about education is that within each of us is a natural striving for independence. We, as adults, choose what we want to learn. The real mastery takes place inside us.

In the classroom there are long, open work periods where the children are choosing the materials they're going to work with. The child is learning about his or her own cycle of work and may work intently for forty-five minutes cleaning a table. A parent might say, 'Wait a minute. I just paid $300 a month so my child can clean a table?' But in the process, there are all kinds of cause-and-effect thinking going on. There's sequencing in getting the pail, filling it with water, knowing how close to put it to the table, and getting the table clean to the point where the child is satisfied with it. My job is to observe the patterns being exhibited. What Montessori talks about has to do with learning and understanding our rhythms, and empowering children to focus and be attentive.

I see myself as a sounding board, a kind and caring person who can reflect something back to them. My students do a lot of journal writing. They all do their family trees, and they research the period in which their family's story took place. It's a time for them to learn about themselves. I really want to know what they're thinking and how they're putting the world together. Especially at their age—eleven to fourteen years old—they go through so many changes, not just in their bodies but in their whole information processing and questioning of their values and of each other. It's fascinating to watch it unfold.

In my class of thirty-six students, I can have a meaningful relationship with each of them. We can sit down, have lunch together, have an interesting conversation about their soccer team or a cotillion or what they're going to do for the summer. These are people I care about. It's hard for me to let go of them. I've been watching many of them grow up since they were three years old. I remember their older brothers and sisters; I remember when their parents stood with tears in their eyes at the curb dropping them off at school. I was once a parent dropping my own kid off at this school.

We're a small community. It's very much a partnership. We don't do grades; we do narrative evaluations and parent conferences, and we have phone or e-mail conferences anytime. It's a great privilege to be able to teach in a situation like this. I have significant relationships that matter. 🙶

"In an important way, I began to discover that the purpose of teaching is change, from a not-knowing to a knowing stage, or in the way that you think about things."

WALLY WOLFE
Psychology Professor
Powell, Wyoming

Change

Change is never easy. For the following teachers, however, it is what drives their teaching. By helping others
and by sharing what they know, these teachers are catalysts
for change in the lives of those around them. They
believe in the power of positive change—they have wit-
nessed its effects in their classrooms and in their lives.
Creating change keeps them actively engaged in teaching
and gives them goals to strive for. For these teachers,
there is pride in even the small transformations they have
effected, and in knowing that in their own way, they are
making their part of the world a better place.

Oveta Anderson

Oveta Anderson is a math resource teacher for grades one through four at the Westminster Schools in Atlanta, Georgia. She has been teaching, mostly in independent schools, for twenty-three years.

❝ I look at my teaching career, and it's been rewarding because I've touched the lives of kids, not only educationally but in a moral sense. I think I've helped them. I feel good about that.

Some students haven't been exposed to a black teacher before—maybe a black housekeeper or gardener, but not someone at the same level as their other teachers. They come into the classroom and here I am! They have to identify with me, and there's value in that. I remember one little girl feeling my skin. She just said it was smooth. I said, 'The only thing different is my pigmentation. It's smooth just like yours.' She said, 'It is.'

It seems like every place I go, I'm the first teacher of color. At one independent school, I was a fifth-grade homeroom teacher, and the parents were a little concerned because they were expecting a white teacher. It was a learning experience for me and for them, and a positive one.

I once applied to teach third grade at an independent school in Richmond, Virginia. Some of the teachers were showing me around, and one of them said, 'If you accept this position, you'll be the Jackie Robinson of the Lower School.' I said, 'I will?' This was 1987–88. I liked the school, the facilities, the people. The minority population was very small. I went home and pondered. I decided to accept the position for the black students who were there, as well as for the faculty. After I accepted, the principal said to me, 'What can we do to make your transition a smooth one?' I asked if she asked that of all her teachers. She said no. I said, 'Why did you ask me?' I thanked her for being sensitive, but told her this was not my first time in this situation. Then I told her that if she felt she needed to discuss the race issue, it would be better to talk to her faculty instead of me.

When I was five years old, my mother and I were walking to the five-and-ten-cent store. We always shopped there. I began to cough as we were walking down the street. My mother said, 'Let's go into the store and get some water.' We did, and they wouldn't give her any water. My mother said, 'She's just a little girl. Can't you give her some water?' At that time, I'm still coughing, and I can remember this big man in a suit came from behind us, and the counter guy said to my mother, 'I think you'd better leave.' So my mother took my hand and we left. She told me we'd be home soon.

That's when my mother first explained what racism was about. A young child can't get water! So when people try to bend over backwards, I take a deep breath and explain that whatever guilt feelings may be going on, those are something that they have to deal with. When I interviewed with Westminster, I asked the principal of the elementary school, 'How many teachers of color have you had?' She came out with 'None.' I went home and said to my husband, 'This must be my calling.'

You get into the teaching profession because you're committed to making a difference. It's not just the planning of a lesson but the way you teach that lesson—the enthusiasm and motivation you give to the students—that's important. You may not always be successful in teaching the lesson. You may have to critique it, edit, and start all over, but that's okay. Even though a lot of teaching is lesson plans and the grading of papers, it's more. You have to be dedicated enough to see that it goes beyond that.

Every day is a new day, and I will be able to touch a student in some way, bring that student out in some way —whether it's in math or has something to do with the student's self-image—because I'm going to expose that student to something new. I enjoy seeing the response I get from children when they realize they'll be able to do something, or they have the ability to learn new skills. That's what keeps me going, the assurance that I'm going to get a response like that from a child. They're going to be more aware of something they did not know before, and it's going to make them feel more positive about who they are and what they're doing. That's why I teach.

Rita Sigrist

Rita Sigrist is the special services instructor at Monett Senior High School in Monett, Missouri. She has been teaching for twenty-two years.

66 I deal on a personal level with each of my students. They know whatever they tell me will be kept confidential. There have been times when I've been the first one they've told when they realize they're pregnant. I've had students come to me weeping that Dad abused them. Probably 75 percent come from broken homes. I feel like my room is an oasis, the one quiet spot in their day. Many times they just want to sit in a corner and talk to me. So it's dealing with students on an individual basis and having to hear about their lives that's the hard part, but it's the part I feel I do best.

I'm finding more and more often that we're getting students who were crack babies or had fetal alcohol syndrome, and many, many who are attention-deficit-hyperactivity disordered. I've lived through it for ten years now with my son. We adopted him as a nineteen-month-old baby from India. The moment I saw him, I said, 'He's gifted . . . and he's behavior-disordered.' My son once had a teacher who told everyone that he was a spoiled brat.

He had been diagnosed by a medical doctor and a psychiatrist. My son has an IQ of 140. Someone who hasn't gone through it can never understand. I become very upset with people who say, 'Oh, I understand.' I'll say, 'Have you lived with an ADD kid for ten years? Then you don't.'

I'm really blunt with some people. As a matter of fact, the older I get, the brassier I get. I'm very proud of that fact.

I can't save my students, but I can teach them to cope and understand cause and effect and consequence. People think we baby-sit them. And we don't. I work very hard with my students. I want them to be able to communicate, both in writing and orally. That's why we talk a lot. When they do their writing, they have to read aloud to a reading partner. It's very hard because their writings are so incredibly personal. Often you don't get out of them what you know is there, and they're embarrassed to read aloud, so they read quietly over in a corner. I have certain students who are good writing partners because they'll say [to the partnering student], 'That was really good; you told me a lot about yourself.' I try so hard to find something that's important to every student and bring it out. Some children think they have nothing good about them.

I have a hard time dealing with people who think that all special-ed kids are—and I hate this word—retarded. I don't allow my students to say that word in my classroom. I've never called my kids 'special ed.'

I come to their defense every chance I get, but [when there are behavior problems] I also stand back and say, 'You're taking responsibility. If you choose to act like this, this is what will happen.' I'm trying to teach them consequence, while still saying, 'I understand exactly how you feel, but you can't do that in public.' I'm always going out of my way to explain to them that I have disabilities, too. All of us do. Some are evident, some are not.

I remember I had a young man who was extremely intelligent. He was doing trigonometry and calculus. I had no idea what it was, but he could not read or write above a second grade level. As long as I read the book to him, as long as I read the test to him, he knew the answers. I would write them down. The mainstream teachers would say, 'Do you tell him the answers?' And I'd say, 'You come in and watch me give him the test.'

Believe me, I'll try anything once to see if it'll work. It's the desire to help somebody live a better life. I got into teaching because I thought you'd get a lot of prestige and three months off—and that's totally false! I work all year long. I work weekends, I work late into the night. But I've had students from fourteen or fifteen years ago come back and bring their children and invite me to their weddings. It's worth every minute that I put in.

Frank Beckendorf

Frank Beckendorf teaches English and reading at Stella Worley Junior High School in Westwego, Louisiana. Before becoming a teacher, he was a police officer for ten years in New Orleans, Louisiana. He has been teaching for six years.

❝ Why I teach is because I enjoy it. I used to teach some law enforcement at a technical school at night. I was thrilled being able to share information with people. Education always stuck in the back of my mind.

In the school I'm teaching in now, we have about eight hundred kids, a mixture of black and white, some Vietnamese and American Indian. We had three kids arrested this year for first-degree murder. Some of the kids come to school in shackles—it's court-ordered; they've been confined to the house and stuff like that. Anytime you try to reach kids like this and help them feel good about themselves, you have to give them some encouragement to do so.

I try to pay attention to what kids are saying. I stay away from front-of-the-room lecturing. What I stress is collaborative and independent learning. Kids will say, 'Mr. B., how do you spell such and such?' I tell them to get a dictionary and look it up. 'Well, how do I look it up if I can't spell it?' I tell them to listen to the word and think of how it might be spelled. I make them look for the answer. They'll say, 'How do I . . . ?' and I'll say, 'Why don't you tell me?'

Kids know I care. Sometimes I can get abrupt. There was one kid who was caught with a stolen car in a neighboring parish. I said to him, 'Why are you doing stupid things?' The kid knows I care about him. He said, 'Well, I'm not going to do it again.' I said, 'I hope not, because you know what's going to happen to you!' We've had kids like that murdered; we've had kids commit suicide.

I had a kid come to me the day before who said, 'Read this in my journal.' It said, 'Mr. B., I know I can't pass, but I think you're a great teacher. I know I can't pass,' he said it again, 'but I don't want to get you next year.' These kids have three Fs on their report card for three quarters, and I'm honest and truthful with them, which they appreciate. I'll say, 'There is nothing you can do to pass. I've been emphasizing this all year long—to get moving, to get motivated. I gave you extra-credit opportunities. You've done nothing, so make plans to be in seventh-grade reading again next year, or summer school.' The kid likes me; he knows I'm fair, and he knows it's his own fault. So guess what. I've taught him a lesson in life. It's a rough lesson to learn.

What I'm trying to say is that the traditional definition of what a teacher does in the classroom is not the way I approach it. With the one hundred fifty kids I have, if I change ten attitudes about reading, then that's a lot of success. If I convince ten kids that reading is great and wonderful and I put good literature in their hands, then my job's done. I have kids out there with five or ten different books they've never heard of. They enjoy reading. They go back to tell their parents and the principal that they love the class. I do a lot of hands-on with those guys. They do a lot of presentations, and they love it.

People still see these old movies where a teacher is in front of a one-room schoolhouse lecturing and kids are writing. Traditionally, that's what the public thinks a teacher is. However, I've had my nose broken twice breaking up fights. You are a mediator, you are a counselor, you are a social worker. You are a mama and a daddy to them. A lot of these kids do not have mothers and fathers.

I have a reading course the last hour of the day with a group of seventh graders who are honor-section kids. I'm trying to instill in them an interest in reading more than just what is forced on them by a teacher. I want them to know that it's okay to pick up a book and if you don't like it, you can pick up something else. If I can't reach them with English-class topics, then I'm trying to tell them about life and society. I've had some kids I've made a difference with. I enjoy trying to reach their minds. I'm successful in some cases. In a lot of cases I'm not, but I'm trying. 🙶

Brian Baute

Brian Baute teaches English. He is a native of Indiana and spent his first year in teaching at Terre Haute South High School in Terre Haute, Indiana. He is currently in his second year at Walter M. Williams High School in Burlington, North Carolina.

❝ I try as much as possible to act out what it means to be a Christian. I'm a strong believer in students' freedom to express themselves in whatever way they choose. When Jesus was on Earth, he wasn't concerned about forming institutions and shoving through laws. He cared for people; he showed them that they mattered and that they could be more than they already were. That's something I strive to do as a teacher, to care about my individual students and to show them that they really are worthwhile. A lot of times, especially in lower-level classes, they don't get that anywhere else.

A lot of times all it takes is showing them that if they get a good grade on their report card, they'll be congratulated. Or maybe even more importantly, if they get a bad grade, someone will hold them accountable. So I try, and I hope I'm at least moderately successful, not to make them believe the way I do, not to agree with me, but just to show them by the way I act that they matter, that they have potential. If nothing else, I hope a lot of these kids can realize, Hey, he's a Christian, but he's not yelling at me. He's not saying you have to wear a shirt and tie all the time or you can't listen to music you like.

One of the demons of first- and second-year teaching is that the biggest rewards are going to be down the road. But I see so many people who look back over what they've done. They might have had a great time doing it, and it might have made them a lot of money, but it didn't change things. I hate to sound too idealistic, but I want to be able to look back and say, 'Yeah, this world, this big ball of dirt, is better because of what I was able to do.' I've always been kind of a closet computer geek, and I started as a computer-science major in college. I could have made a lot of cash! But it wouldn't have made a difference. Maybe I would have designed the next big chip after the Pentium. Maybe I'd have made $13 billion! But I don't think anyone like Bill Gates is really improving the world. You improve the world by improving the people in the world, one person at a time. There is a place for national, international, and global things, but when it comes down to nuts and bolts, it's got to be individuals. And teaching is one of the best ways to do that.

From a global perspective, one little crummy second-year teacher doesn't matter. But when you're able to intercede for others as a teacher—ask for help, for guidance, for healing—it has a very strong effect. 🙶

Kathy Ross

Kathy Ross teaches sixth-grade science and reading and eighth-grade Spanish at Stone Middle School in Wiggins, Mississippi. She has also taught math. She has been teaching for nineteen years.

❝ I teach in a very rural area, about thirty miles from the Gulf of Mexico. Most of my students have farmlike chores on small plots of family-owned land. Wiggins is sort of unique for a small town in Mississippi because the schools are better than in some of the other parts of the state. We have a lot of children whose parents are not well educated. I had one student several years back who had trouble with math, and her mother said she only had about a fourth-grade education herself in math. I told the student to go home and teach her mom what she'd learned in school, and that seemed to work quite well.

One of the best things about Wiggins is that the people here just seem to have an interest in education. I grew up in Illinois, and the impression I had of Mississippi was that there were a lot of barefoot people running around who were very poor and not well educated. The fact is there's a lot of intellect among the people who live in the Gulf Coast area. Our students win awards in science fairs, and our marching band is the best in the state. We're getting computers in every classroom this year, and we already have several computer labs. We're one of the only towns in Mississippi that has so much technology.

When I first moved here, the kids thought I was from a foreign country. I couldn't understand their speech and they couldn't understand mine. They asked me which country I was from and I told them Illinois. I don't think the schools were as good then as they are now. The school district decided they wanted improvement, and so they started having the kids write. I was glad I taught math, because you just couldn't make any sense out of what the kids were writing. But we've come a long way, and their writing has really improved.

I was in the Army for a short time, mostly as a Korean linguist. The kids think it's really neat. I was playing softball for a church team and some of the kids started calling me Senior Master Sergeant. I said, 'Well, I was a Senior Master Sergeant!' They thought they were picking on me and said they didn't know that was my rank. Sometimes when I'm teaching, I wish I could tell them to drop down and do twenty pushups. I mentioned that to some of them toward the end of last year, and they couldn't wait to show me how many pushups they could do! They didn't want to be punished; they just wanted to do them for fun.

Teaching people is helping them. I like to help people and to share. Anything I learn to do I want to share with everybody else—not just the kids. We had an in-service class last year, and the teacher sitting next to me at the computer had absolutely no computer skills at all. She was afraid of the mouse. But I helped her, and she was willing to learn. I'm constantly learning as well through teaching. 🙶🙶

Rachel Sheeley

*Rachel Sheeley teaches fourth grade at Edwardsville
Elementary School in Edwardsville, Kansas. She has been
teaching for eight years.*

❝ I grew up on a small dairy farm outside Nortonville,
Kansas. We had dairy cows, sometimes as many as seventy-five or more. My sister and I helped with the field work
as well as milking and taking care of all the animals. My
mother is an educator, but she kept discouraging me
because she knew how hard teachers worked and how little pay they received.

I went to Kansas State University and took up what I
hoped would be a degree in veterinary medicine. It didn't
work out, and after working at the vet school at the
University for several years, I kept thinking, This really
isn't what I want to do. While I was there, the person I
worked under taught a toxicology class to the senior
veterinary students. I helped him from time to time,
which kept me thinking I really wanted to get back into
teaching.

It helps me as a teacher to have a strong background in
a rural community. I participated in a lot of things growing up on my family's farm. What led me to vet school was
probably my fascination with how to take care of the animals when they were sick. Being a small farm, we did as
much of our own veterinary work as we could. I think the
whole idea of family farming is really a learning and teach-

ing process, too, because we had to teach other family members or people in the community how we do things.

People still tell me I could be doing so much more than teaching. I say, 'But I don't think I would be happy. I tried and I know it doesn't work.' It takes a certain type of person to be a teacher. You can almost pick teachers out of a crowd or in a group of people talking, just by their actions and how they relate to others. I see it, anyway.

I teach in a lower-income area. Some of the parents don't have a high-school education, and a high percentage are on welfare. So, realizing that some of the children's lives leave a lot to be desired and that we as teachers can somehow change that a little bit, makes you go back every day. It's also the little notes the children give to you, and the little hugs. And knowing that I've had former students track me down after I've moved. And that ten years down the road, my mom has former students coming up to her and saying how she made them want to change their lives. Those are the things that make you think, Wow, I'm doing something that's really important. 99

Karen Gotwald

Karen Gotwald teaches seventh-grade reading at Roxboro Middle School in Cleveland Heights, Ohio. She works with children who have lower-level reading skills, drawing on her own experiences with a reading disability. She has made over eighty presentations of a program she designed called Crises—Helping Kids Cope! which uses children's picture books to encourage and support teachers, parents, and other adults who want to help children of all ages express their feelings. She has been teaching for twenty-six years.

66 Once I got in the door of teaching kids, I was able to be who I was. I'd never read a picture book aloud until I was in front of second graders, because I was too self-conscious. But what I learned about reading aloud is that you're allowed to read slower and you can make it expressive.

Crises—Helping Kids Cope! began when I was teaching second grade. It was one of those things I was willing to risk doing because I didn't know any better. Second graders were walking into my class and telling me things that were painful or troubling, and I wasn't able to ignore them. When a pet died, or a grandmother, or somebody was sick, there was no way I could say, 'Open your math book to page twenty-eight.'

I ordered a series of children's picture books from a book club and began to read them aloud to my class. The books dealt with death, divorce, where babies come from, disabilities, and other issues. I realized that if a little person had a pain he or she was willing to talk about, there was probably more than one such child in the class. My whole philosophy is that pain is very isolating, but that if a person knows that somebody else has been through something similar, perhaps it won't be so painful.

Adults often leave kids out of a crisis, which usually makes kids build it up to be much bigger and scarier. What I try to share with adults is that, even though they may be feeling vulnerable about their self-control and own emotional levels, why not share that with kids? Why would adults want kids to learn that it's not okay to have difficult times and to share them with people we love? That's usually who's around.

I never say anything that people don't already know. What I do is remind them of common-sense things we lose sight of. I'm giving them reminders about being kind and human and open. If we can simplify things and look at real lessons, they're usually much easier than we think. It's also easier to talk about them in picture-book form, because it's less intimidating.

We can't walk away from the idea that kids are willing to share whatever is going on in their lives. We have to be present for them. We don't have to know the answers. There isn't a way to fix so many of the things they bring us, but we can certainly look a child in the eye and have the compassion to say, 'I'm here for you if you need me.' Often that's all they need to know. You're not going to reach the kids you work with, no matter what age, if you're not willing to treat them with respect and dignity. We're the adults and they're the kids—so we need to go the extra mile in terms of making it work. As the professionals, if the dignity and the respect aren't there, it's our job to create them.

My reading disability is probably what's helped me with the kinds of kids I'm working with. If I hadn't experienced what it feels like to struggle with everything, I don't think I'd be as positively involved. I'm not going to save the world, which I believed I would when I started twenty-six years ago. But once in a while a kid cracks a joke in reaction to something I'm saying or doing, and I can roll with it. That's really where I am as a teacher. Kids do or say something each day that brightens my day. And I pay attention to that, because that's what teaching's all about. 🙶

Bill Burrall

Bill Burrall teaches computer and technology literacy at Moundsville Junior High School in Moundsville, West Virginia. He has been nationally recognized for his work integrating technology into the school curriculum. The Inmates and Alternatives Project, an ongoing, online dialogue between his students and prisoners, is archived in the Smithsonian Museum. He has been teaching for twenty-six years.

66 I got involved with technology back in the early 1980s. I had some classroom projects going on the Internet. A lot of people are surprised to hear that, and to hear that the Internet is twenty-five years old. It really caught my eye as to what we could do with classroom/technology integration.

I entered the public school system as a French and social studies teacher. When I got involved with technology, there were no courses; there were no other teachers; there were no professors who taught what we needed to know. Back then we learned it from the ground up. I was the person who displayed the interest in it. I took that first step and, hence, I ended up with all of it in my lap, good and bad. I find that a lot of friends who got started in technology back then—band directors, musicians, people who teach across the curriculum—are the people who more or less got in on the ground floor. Once they learned it, they were in such demand that they practically had no choice but to become the college teachers or to take adjunct professorships and teach the technology to other teachers. I continually do so, and I still have no degree in it.

Inmates and Alternatives started because we used to have a classroom building four blocks from West Virginia's state penitentiary. I had the idea of having modem access, and the prison education department had an online bulletin board that we could link into. It snowballed, and we got other schools involved across the United States and around the world. One of the most important things that came out of it was that kids heard responses from inmates such as, 'I thought I knew everything, and I found out I knew nothing.' 'I made wrong decisions.' You also have to look at whether inmates can use technology for rehabilitation. For example, one of the inmates involved has been released on parole. He recently started up a business as an ISP [Internet service provider].

It's a situation where I continually try to keep up [with technology], and I can't even begin to approach where I feel I need to be. There are a lot of different views on this stuff. Some people take the approach that if I learn it and don't share my knowledge, I'll have job security. I think that's a shame. There are people out there like that. Then there are some who will share anything; I consider myself one of those.

If I were to go back into the traditional French or social studies classroom, I would wither up and die if they didn't give me computers to teach with. It's the constant flux and change of technology that really makes it exciting. I teach different things every year, because it changes that quickly. I now have teleconferencing I can do; I've got all these applications and new CD-ROMs that are out, which are more exciting for kids to use than the textbook. I'm not saying they're meant to replace the textbook, but sitting there reading chapters, answering questions, and listening to a classroom lecture can't hold a candle to visiting a site on the 'Net.

Students like it because it's immediate feedback. They're always busy with their hands; the old adage that idle hands are a problem is true. If kids have interactive technologies available to them, they can find information within seconds, whereas it might take them hours or days to look it up in a library.

So I think it's the constant change that keeps me going, and the new things that are appearing on our horizon, and the things we haven't even considered that, in the next five or ten years, are just going to knock our socks off. ""

Wally Wolfe

Wally Wolfe is an assistant professor of psychology at Northwest College, a liberal arts community college in Powell, Wyoming. He is also a counseling psychologist. He has been teaching for thirteen years.

❝ I trained to be a clinician. I didn't think I'd ever teach. I was working as a forensic psychologist in South Carolina. The job I had was grant funded, and like many grants, ours was shaky. I went out to find another job and was hired to teach general psychology at a technical college. Something happened when I went into the classroom; I knew that was where I was supposed to be.

What I understand about my field is continually fascinating to me. Apparently that gets communicated, because I get a lot of comments about it from students. It's a 'Gee, look what I found!' kind of thing, a small boy's pleasure in showing off his shiny new rock.

I think education is ultimately a relationship issue. You can get all the facts you ever need off the Internet (some of them aren't right, but they're there). You can always look stuff up in a book, but the processes of thinking, the ways of thinking, and our general approach to thinking tend to come out of some kind of interpersonal relationship. That's carryover from my clinical training—because we were taught for years that the most important element of the therapeutic relationship was the relationship itself, not the orientation or the specific techniques the therapist used.

Community colleges have a way of doing this, because the emphasis is on teaching. Anybody who's managed to get a GED can walk in. Most of the students haven't got a clue how to do college work. So when you work with them and they master things, you get a real sense of accomplishment. I once talked with a guy who had taught at MIT [Massachusetts Institute of Technology] and quit his job there to go down the road to a community college. He said the reason was that those guys at MIT didn't need him. They were going to learn anyway. The folks at a community college need somebody.

One of the hardest things I've done is teach night classes. You start at six o'clock, and you're grumpy and tired. But you go in and you get increased energy, at least I do. Then the class ends and everybody walks out together, and then you do the parking lot seminar that goes on for another hour. It's eleven o'clock by the time you get home, and you can't sleep because you're energized by the ideas you've been talking about and the relationships you've been having. While it occasionally costs you some sleep, it sure feels good.

My role is pretty clearly defined in a classroom. As a therapist, it's not. One of the nice things about teaching is you're in charge for that hour. What I do in the classroom is known to me and my students and to nobody else. It's a place where I can order the material and profess to know what's important. I can work with it to make it tell a story.

I noticed after the first year that what I was doing was actually helping people to change. Part of the change was because I was teaching [the subject of] psychology. But I thought about how the purpose of therapy is change. In an important way I began to discover that the purpose of *teaching* is change, from a not-knowing to a knowing stage, or in the way that you think about things. I'm not trying to do therapy in the classroom, but you can go in and teach about how people make certain kinds of cognitive errors and have thirty people hear it, and maybe ten of them pick it up and won't need a therapist later on. So teaching and therapy begin to connect like that for me.

Teaching is really kind of like gambling, because you never know when you're going to get your payoff. I'll work with the students for a couple of years, they'll take two or three of my classes, and then they'll disappear. Every few years one of them comes back and says, 'I'm in this graduate program' or 'I've started three Ph.D.'s.' Every once in a while you'll get a payoff, and you just go back in and do it some more. If you intermittently reward the rat, he will press the bar steadily and continuously forever and forever. 🙶🙶

"Teaching is the only job you'll ever have where you get up in the morning and you don't know what's going to happen."

GLORIA RAMSEY
Science Teacher
Memphis, Tennessee

Surprise

Like life, teaching is filled with unexpected struggles and rewards. For the following teachers, the element of surprise is one of the things that make teaching meaningful. They are surprised by what their students do and say in class, and by former students who return to thank them. They are surprised by unexpected moments, sometimes moments of awareness and maturity in students that transcend their ages. And they are surprised by themselves, by how their perspectives change over time, and by how much they continue to learn as teachers. Ultimately, teaching offers one surprise after another for these teachers.

Mary Helen Cholka

Mary Helen Cholka teaches sixth-grade English and science at William D. Slider Middle School in El Paso, Texas. She has been teaching for twenty-three years.

❝ I came out of a bilingual household in El Paso, where both English and Spanish were spoken. My mom spoke Spanish and my dad spoke English. I don't remember not speaking both languages. When I got into first grade, the teacher was a tall, thin, big-boned woman who hated Spanish speakers. I guess I sensed it. I didn't want to be in school. To her I would only speak Spanish. To the Spanish teacher—they taught foreign language at the time—I would only speak English. I was not a cooperative child.

I think educators, whether we're teachers in the classroom or administrators, are viewed as, 'Oh, well, they couldn't do anything else in life, so they taught.' National Teachers' Week is also Be Kind to Your Pet Week! I chose of my own free will to teach. It wasn't because I couldn't cut it in the business world.

When people say, 'What do you teach?' and I say I teach middle school, they start asking why. 'Why don't you teach the little ones?' Or, 'Why don't you teach high school?' Well, if I wanted to teach elementary or high school I would have. I'm happy in the middle, with everything that comes with puberty. I feel puberty is contagious. These poor kids at the middle-school level are so confused. Their bodies are changing. Things are growing, things are developing and happening, and—I'm guilty of this sometimes with my own children—adults say, 'Act like a young adult!' But the minute these kids go out and show any independence that we don't like, it's, 'No, no, you're a little kid.'

Middle school is the time when they're social. They're not there for the education. We know that, but we force them. We try to force them to sit at a desk. We try by saying, 'You're in class, be quiet.' Their minds are on, How do I look? Where's my biggest pimple? How can I remove it? This is where these kids learn how to act, how to become 'adults.' Overall, they're good kids. To me, all kids are good. Some of them get involved in things that are bad, but how many of us did? Some of us choose not to remember or acknowledge it. We need to remember what *we* did.

I split my junior-high years between a public school and a Catholic school. Sister Jacquelyn would line up all of us girls against the wall and measure our skirts with a yardstick. As far as I was concerned, her name was Sister Jackass. The minute she turned her back, we hauled our skirts up! Now as adults, many teachers say, 'We never did that.' Give me a break! How many of us ditched classes? I didn't pass algebra my freshman year because I was never there. We choose to conveniently forget our middle- or high-school years.

I'm one of those big kids who does things for reactions. It's like, What's going to happen in class today? What can I set up to watch happen? What are they going to set up to watch happen? You can't do that in a court of law. You can't do that as a nurse or a doctor. You can do it with kids.

If I'd been a computer major or an accountant, would I have ever seen seven groups of kids who were tied up as part of a puzzle try to untie themselves—actually watch them figure it out and learn from the process? You need to give kids credit. I never know from the start of one class period to the end what's going to happen. 🙶

Dave Abrahamson

Dave Abrahamson teaches ninth-grade English at Totem Junior High School in Federal Way, Washington. He also coaches basketball, track, and fast-pitch softball. He has been teaching for eight years.

66 I was a pretty poor student—Cs and Ds mostly. I goofed around a lot and was the class clown. After I got out of school, I moved to Los Angeles. I went to film school. A friend and I wrote a screenplay about junior-high kids who start a gambling casino. We seemed close to selling the screenplay, but the bottom line from studios was, 'We don't think we can make money with it. Once you finish your next one, bring it to us.' Having spent a year on that one, it didn't seem like a good return to me. I had always leaned toward working with kids; I got involved in teaching and coaching at a private school and enjoyed it.

One of the main things I stress in classes is, 'There's no *I* in *teams*.' We talk about what that means. The kids come to the conclusion that somebody's making decisions for the team. But then we talk about making sure the team you're part of is going in the direction you want. Do you want to be part of Nazi Germany and not ask questions? Or do you have the strength to say, 'I'm going to stand alone by myself'? It's a wonderful lesson in junior high, because then we talk about what kind of clothes they wear and why they wear them. What happens if you like a different music group than everybody else? How do you treat people who are different?

The one issue that junior-high kids face every day is fitting into a group. That's a tough thing for them; they're all dealing with it. They think, If I could just look like her, or him, or be the star player, my problems would be solved. As we get older and beaten down by real-life experiences, we come to realize that everybody has problems. Everybody is not delighted, and that's okay. There's nothing like a good ten- or twenty-year class reunion to open your eyes a little.

A junior-high kid makes such a point of saying what's stupid and what they've outgrown. At the same time, I've taken them several times to Dairy Queen or McDonald's, and they're all too happy to go out on the playground area like they're ten years old. Although they seem to be grown up, they're incredible kids inside. They have a lot of positive energy, and they want to learn, as much as they say they don't and resist it. There have been several occasions in our school when teachers have been pretty laid back and the kids complained; they want to be challenged.

When we start discussing a novel in class and look at it philosophically, it's beautiful to see that growth in them, to see them thinking that hard. I'll see them in the lunch room that same day and we'll sit down and talk about a book for quite a while—it's wonderful. The last two years we've studied *One Flew over the Cuckoo's Nest*. It tends to be a book that isn't looked at until senior year in high school. They get very frustrated. They complain a lot and tell me they don't understand it. But it always surprises me that they stress how much they learned at the end, and how important it is to study that book. That's the great thing about teaching. Every day is a surprise. 🙶

Cordenia Paige

Cordenia Paige teaches second grade at Georgetown Day School (GDS), an independent kindergarten-through-twelfth-grade school, in Washington, DC. She also attended the school as a student. She has been teaching there for eight years.

66 People ask me, 'Why don't you teach in a public school?' What I really like about GDS is that it's a little more relaxed. It's probably one of the most nontraditional of the independent schools. I can wear a T-shirt and shorts to teach in. A lot of people say that if you don't look professional, people won't treat you professionally. I don't think that's true. I'm not saying you should be sloppy—but when I walk into that classroom and have a concept to teach, it doesn't matter what I'm wearing. It's how I present it. That's what makes it professional.

Too often we get hung up on the superficial instead of what's really happening. When visitors come to the school, one thing that takes them aback is that it seems so relaxed. But when they really get a chance to see what the kids are doing, they see that we've got second graders studying and writing reports on Inuits and Native Americans. The kids teach the parents about them when they go home! That's kind of exciting. It's funny, too, to see that the kids want to be in school, no matter what the weather's like. And I wonder, what are we doing to these kids that they want to be there everyday? But most days, I want to be there, too.

One thing I'm proud of as a teacher is that I feel flexible. I don't really have a rhythm; I often pick it up from the kids. As a student, I was considered quiet because I didn't like to talk in front of a group. I still remember being terrified in college when I had to take a speech class. But it's fun to get up in front of kids, because they're such an eager audience. Friends of mine who work nine to five ask, 'Why are you so tired after work?' And I think, I'm performing every day. What makes me love it is that you don't know what these little human beings are going to say. They come up with something hilarious or really profound, and you're like, 'That came from you?'

Sometimes we get caught up in what needs to get done. We have a curriculum and certain projects we have to do throughout the year, and you get in the mode that you don't have time for fun. But you also have to step back and say, What's really going to be lost if we don't do this particular project—or if it's not done this particular way? It's a constant balancing act. I've started trying to learn juggling as a result. My thinking is, Maybe if I get better at juggling *physically*. . . . I know a lot of teachers who have taken up something else to teach them a sense of balance.

You have to learn that richness is more than just financial. There's a richness in the types of people that I meet, and in the fact that in teaching, the human part is put first. I worked in the corporate world for about a year, and it really bothered me when someone would call in sick and the rest of the office would say, 'Oh, her kids are sick again.' Well, it happens; as teachers, we know it comes with the territory. Kids are going to get sick. Sometimes teachers have to be out because their own kids get sick. Or their spouses are doing something and they need to go, too. That kind of understanding is given a lot of value in teaching, and I like that. 🙦🙦

Jeff Johnston

Jeff Johnston teaches biology, meteorology, oceanography, and endangered species at Pau-Wa-Lu Middle School in Gardnerville, Nevada. In 1997 he was selected as Nevada's State Teacher of the Year in conjunction with the U.S. Department of Education. He has been teaching for seventeen years.

66 The rewards in teaching are profound. It's difficult to find a job where you're in front of a group of people every day and able to see the impact you're making. There's an intrinsic reward to that. I've had jobs where you sit behind a desk and you're pushing a lot of paper around, and you really don't have a clue if what you're doing is making any difference to anybody. In teaching, it's not that way. I've also been in some jobs where once you get the hang of it, it's pretty routine. In teaching, it never becomes routine.

Science is a natural hook for kids, especially the bizarre stuff that goes on. There have been a lot of events in the news relating to biology—like the cloning of sheep—that kids are interested in. If you can get them to say, 'That's really interesting; I want to know why that works,' then you can go forward because they want to learn it at a much deeper level. I have no illusions that the kids who leave my class are going to be junior biologists or oceanographers, but twenty years down the road, if they come across an article about something, they can be literate enough within science to read it and explain it to somebody else. That, to me, is really the goal of an educator anyway—to make people literate in whatever topic you're teaching.

You can't get too cocky. You've got to continue looking at what you do with a critical eye. There are days when I come home and go, 'I wasn't on top of things today,' and I get mad at myself. I think you've got to keep doing that if you don't want to stagnate within the profession.

My first year of teaching was in an eighth-grade science class. It was maybe two months into the year that a kid transferred out. He wasn't doing that badly; he wasn't a bad kid or a troublemaker. When I asked him why he was leaving—and I made the mistake of doing this in front of all the kids—he said, 'I'm going to a class where I can learn something.' I remember the kids in that room turning and looking at my reaction. That was the most painful arrow he could have shot at me. I must have looked really disheartened, because later that day several kids came up to me and said, 'Don't pay any attention to him. He was angry, and there's something else going on in his life.' But it was a comment that really stayed with me. It made me sit down and think, Are these kids learning anything?

I think the more you teach, the more realistic you get about recognizing that when you have a kid who says something like that, you can't ignore it, but you have to understand that maybe you're having a bad day or a bad week and things just aren't coming together the way you want. Those days are easier to deal with simply because you know they don't last forever. This year there were a couple of first-year teachers who would come into my classroom after school and say, 'I've had it! I'm going to work in the produce section!' You've got to explain to them that this is not an ongoing pattern. You have to think about a day that went well, and say that it's going to happen again.

Something like that happened to me last year. It was the end of soccer season. We were having a pizza party with all the kids. I scanned the restaurant and I recognized a girl who was a student I'd had a number of years ago. I smiled at her. A few minutes later her husband came up to me. He introduced himself and said, 'I've just got to meet you.' He told me that his wife had talked about me a lot. She had graduated from college and had a secondary teaching credential. She'd told her husband that I was the sole reason she'd gone into teaching, that I'd motivated her to that extent. They were leaving the next morning for Arizona. She'd gotten a teaching position there.

He didn't realize how important it was to me that he said that, and how humbling. There aren't many professions in which you have people coming up and telling you what a tremendous impact you made on them. 🙶🙶

Susie Gravel

Susie Gravel teaches kindergarten at the Wayne Elementary School in Wayne, Maine. Before becoming a teacher she worked in health care. She has taught kindergarten for eleven years.

❝ Kindergarten is a real high-energy kind of job. I get an incredible range of abilities and developmental skills. Hopefully what happens is I bring those who have very few skills closer to those who have great skills. I've already got kids doing reading, which I don't teach them. And while one kid's doing cartwheels in the group circle, another one's sitting there wishing he could get to the table and write because he already knows how. And another one doesn't even want to pick up a crayon; he wants to romp around and move. So there's a lot of balancing. You have to make sure you're giving the movers enough time, and the ones who are ready to sit enough time to feel like they're accomplishing something, too.

In many areas of the country there's a real academic push at kindergarten. I don't happen to believe in that. I read to them; they act out stories. We do a lot of cooking, and experiential stuff around letter sounds. They're still so young, and they still need so much play time. There's a great deal of complexity in kindergarten. And the thing that scares me a little is that people are nervous about allowing it to just be play. Kids learn so much through play!

We have a garden project going in back of the school. Last week I started a lesson by asking, 'How many parts does a plant have?' And this one little boy whispered to a friend, 'It's four.' The possible answers were one, two, three, and four. I had a slew of kids say 'two' because all you can see so far of the plants we planted are the stem and the leaf. Lots of the kids were actually looking at their plants in the garden. And this little boy whispers, 'It's four. Don't you remember? There's stuff under the ground.' So I had two answers of 'four' because those two children didn't share the information with anybody else!

The lesson that day was pulling the plant apart. I had planted extra bean plants so we could see the roots, see where the stem and the leaves started, and then we talked about what part was missing. And they said, 'The fruit or the bean,' and I said, 'The bean starts as a flower.' So when I asked the question at the end of the day, they all said 'four.' So this one little boy says, 'I knew it! I knew it!' It was a great opportunity for him. He had taught the other little boy about it, and he had explained why.

You have to love kids, and you have to love working with kids, because they are a challenge. You wonder if you make a difference on a daily basis, but when you hear them telling somebody else how to do something, or sharing their knowledge, that's just kind of neat. I guess that's probably what keeps me going. I really love kids and all they can accomplish, and I love watching them grow.

Jim Robinson

Jim Robinson has taught music and drama at schools in New Hampshire, Massachusetts, and New York. He is a native of New Hampshire and most recently has been the principal of Unity Elementary School in Unity, New Hampshire. In 1994 he received a doctorate in education from Harvard University. He has been teaching for thirty-seven years.

66 When I started college, I had no intention of teaching. I wanted to go as a music major, as a performer. That was frowned upon by everybody. I was advised by my high-school guidance counselor that I should major in the sciences, preferably physics, and that I would have a wonderful career and be very rich. I went to college as a physics major, then switched to English. I stopped going to classes for a while and dropped out. When I was ready, I went back as a music major. I did what I wanted to do in the first place, which was to perform. I began to have faint thoughts of, Maybe I'd like to teach a little bit. It would be a good safeguard. I decided that what I wanted to be was a music-education major. Eventually I found out that I'd really rather teach.

I don't fit the mold of principal very well. Too often administrators under pressure think they need to show they're in charge and to rule to some extent by fear. I don't think you gain much by fear in the teaching business. My thinking about how you handle people, particularly people as complex as teachers, is you have to find ways to allow them to do their best. You have to place them in situations where their strengths are recognized and they have a chance to use them.

That's the same way kids learn best. The best teachers I ever had allowed me the opportunity to do things on my own. Kids need to be able to explore some things, if only to find out what went wrong. They need to fail some of the time—not when somebody has forced them into a situation where they've *got* to learn, but when they try to explore something and don't get the right answer. They may learn something anyway.

Fifteen- and sixteen-year-olds can do things that they'll never do again in their lives. There's that wonderful combination of good mind, energy, and naiveté that can take them to a special point. As a teacher, you can give them that opportunity. Some of the most exciting moments in my life have been when they've achieved things far beyond adults or professionals in the same field. I'm sure anybody who reads that would say, 'That guy must have had a terrible life!' But it's not true.

I remember doing *Fiddler on the Roof.* It was a great trial and tribulation. We lost the stage area in the school, and we needed more space. Every night, in order to do the rehearsal, we would build the entire stage in the gymnasium. It took two hours. We would rehearse for two hours, and then we'd take it down again and put it away until there was no trace of it. And we did it three days a week for six or seven weeks. Finally, we did the show and recorded it. A couple of years later, one of the students who'd been in the show was in college in Boston, and he came up to New Hampshire to do a lecture on electronic music. I gave him a ride back and dropped him off where he was living. I walked in with him, and I could hear this tape of *Fiddler on the Roof* playing. His roommate said, 'I just found this tape. Where'd you get it? This is a fantastic recording.' I could see the tape, and I knew which one it was. And the student said, 'That's my high-school production.'

Those things can happen at very strange times. But they're just wonderful moments and you always think, Well, there are going to be a few more of them. 99

Gloria Ramsey

Gloria Ramsey has taught every grade from third through twelfth. She is currently on assignment with the Urban Systemic Initiative (USI) in Memphis, Tennessee. The Memphis USI is a collaboration between the school district and National Science Foundation to improve math and science skills among teachers and students. In 1994 she was a Presidential Awardee in elementary science for the state of Tennessee. She has been teaching for twenty-two years.

66 When I went to high school in the 1960s, girls weren't 'supposed to do' science and math. In my geometry class, the teacher totally ignored us. She actually told me that I was wasting my time in geometry and needed to do something else. I loved science, but until I got involved in a science improvement program for teachers in 1986, I believed I couldn't do it. The city of Memphis was trying to put science labs in all of the elementary schools, and they wanted teachers to volunteer to go back to school for science training. We had to take fifteen hours of upper-level courses. I took physics, chemistry, earth science, biology, and astronomy. I thought, I can do this! And my kids can, too. It became almost a mission for me to show that anybody can learn math and science.

Realizing I could do it was a major hurdle. That's the way I approach it with a lot of teachers. I do the work with them; I let them see they can do it, and then I ask them to try it on their own. I'll come back later and ask, 'How did it go?' They realize that they don't have to know science. They can learn it with their students, and that makes them part of the learning community in their classrooms. It becomes more fun. I worked with a lady who said, 'I don't know how to do this.' She's now the lead science teacher at her school. It's just giving them a sense of, You can do it— you have that ability. You can't make a mistake in science because whatever you do, you learn from it and go on.

Elementary teachers are the love of my heart. We have summer institutes for them. One week we had five hundred elementary teachers come; the next week we had six hundred. If they think they can glean something to make their classrooms more fun, they'll come. It's that cycle of learning we all go through—meeting a challenge and learning from it and meeting the next challenge. I think that's an important part of teaching.

Teaching is the only job you'll ever have where you get up in the morning and you don't know what's going to happen. Whatever does happen, you know you've affected a child's life. I've had kids come back and give me a hug and say, 'Remember when we did this?' That's what makes teaching the most wonderful profession in the world. The children feel better for having been a part of your life, and you feel better for having been a part of theirs. It's never the same any day, or even any hour, from class to class and from child to child. It always invokes a sense of mystery and wonder that can't be found in any other profession. 99

"The thing that makes teaching an adventure is the difficulty. It wouldn't be an adventure if it didn't have some kind of danger or uncertainty or risk."

KATIE SULLIVAN
Elementary Teacher
Warren, Vermont

Adventure

There is an excitement to teaching, a kinetic charge that some teachers feel about their subject matter or when they walk into a school or a classroom. Excitement, challenge, and adventure are three of the things that keep the following teachers going. These teachers are energized by the risk-taking element of their experiences. For some, the physical adventures they have outside the classroom directly affect what they do inside the classroom. These teachers look forward to the challenge of trying to educate their students, as well as the thrill and satisfaction they experience when things go well.

Linda Selvig

Linda Selvig teaches grade nine honors-level earth science at Centennial High School in Boise, Idaho. She is president of the National Earth Science Association for Teachers. She has been teaching for nineteen years.

❝❝ I try to instill in my students that the outdoors, the earth, is their classroom. They can find answers to their questions by looking around them—at the ground, the mountains, the stars. Earth science is an all-encompassing science. You have to know chemistry, physics, geology, and meteorology. When a big storm comes rolling in, we clear out of the classroom and go outside to watch it. We talk about it. What other type of class can you do that in? We go outside and watch huge snowflakes fall. To me, that's why earth science is important. It's something that's every day, whether you're on vacation or in your backyard looking up at the night sky.

I love sharing my life and my experiences with my students. That's why I teach. I was in Pasadena, California, during the Mars Pathfinder landing. I was part of what was called the Education Outreach for the Mars Pathfinder. There were thirteen teachers who got to be with the scientists, talk with them, and just get all kinds of information to bring back to the classroom. In 1986 I was part of the Mount St. Helens Project. A group of teachers was flown down into the crater by helicopter. We were able to walk around inside the volcano and up to the new lava dome that was forming. I've also gone to the Florida Keys to study marine biology and to Alaska to climb glaciers. These are the kinds of things I get to do as a science teacher. When I share my slides with my students, they go, 'Wow! You know what you're talking about.'

I try to make sure my students understand that science is not just a bunch of facts. You need to have a basic background, and from there you ask questions and try to figure out what's going on. Science can't explain everything. As they're growing up, through elementary school, students are always told what the answer should be when they're doing a lab or activity. When they get to the math, they ask me, 'Is my answer right?' I say, 'If your data show that, then it's a valid answer.' 'Yeah,' they say, 'but is it right?' I say, 'Look at what everybody else got. Figure out whether you think your answer is valid.' It's really tough for them; they keep waiting for me to give them the correct answer. Pretty soon they understand. They'll say, 'I'll go talk to the other group and see if they got the answer.' Then you'll start seeing bickering back and forth. This is what science is; you discuss the answers. They're doing what I want them to do when they say, 'I got the right answer and you didn't.'

Teaching is an adventure to me—for example, trying to figure out how I'm going to get a concept across. Last year I didn't have any problem; this year they're not understanding it. What am I doing wrong? How can I change? How can I make them excited?

I do poetry for the kids. I do rap. I sing. I dance. I like to be the person who can give them a chance to learn new things and not be afraid to ask questions. I've been in the business a long time. I think one of the reasons I don't get burnout is I do all these things outside the classroom just so I can say, 'I've done that!' Teachers need to do things and feel that their teaching sparks, excites, and challenges them.🙶🙶

Betty Bozick

Betty Bozick teaches a fifth-and-sixth-grade-combined class at St. Anthony's School in Casa Grande, Arizona. She also taught for seven years on the San Carlos Apache Indian reservation in San Carlos, Arizona. She has been teaching for over thirty years.

❝ I don't think I'd want to be teaching if it weren't challenging. I look forward to making a difference. I don't know why I feel I can make a difference, but for some reason I think I can. I have to leave something on this earth so people will know I was here. If one child in five years suddenly remembers me and remembers what I said to them—'keep going, stick to it, don't give up, try it again'—it's worth everything.

I really went into teaching by accident. I was married and had a family. My fifth child became critically ill. She had brain damage, just overnight. I was due to have my sixth baby. My life was totally at a standstill. I was married to an alcoholic, and things were not good at home. After I had the baby, the doctor suggested that I do some home studies or something to get my mind off the children. He said, 'Why don't you take night classes at the university?' So that's exactly what I did. I would take one course a semester, then two courses, then four courses, and finally I was going year-round. It took me six years.

San Carlos is about eighty miles from Phoenix. The students there were not submissive. They were the opposite. They would hold their heads down with their hair over their eyes. When I first started, I would get down on my knees and look up at them. One boy said to me, 'You are rude.' I asked him why. He said, 'You look at me, and we are not to look at you.' He said eye contact was something they considered impolite. They didn't do it until they were sure of you. We used to feel skins. They would put my hand on their arms and we would compare skin. It was just amazing. I've never had anything like that before with children.

Some of their grandparents, parents, or uncles would come in the classroom drunk and sit on the floor. They would sit there all day, and nobody paid any attention to them. Apache parents had a lot of regard for the teachers. They thought it was a safe place for their children, and they wanted them to be there. I learned to accept them and not think anything about it.

Many of the students would tell me, 'We don't want you here. You're trying to make us different than what we are. We don't want to be different.' I have an Apache dictionary, which is unusual because one of the men who worked on it said it's not supposed to be published. He didn't want other people to learn their language. They are very proud people. It was different from what I'd ever heard and read; but once you found that you fit into their way of life, you listened to them.

Even on playground duty, some of the older boys would say, 'Don't let the children walk in circles around you. That's a bad omen.' They were very superstitious. I honored their superstitions even though I didn't know about them. I tried to be their guest, because I was on their land and I felt I was the minority. A couple of my aides made me camp dresses, which are beautiful. They take about nine yards of material. They didn't do things like that for everyone.

The value system [in Catholic school] is different, but again, this is a challenge for me. I rely a lot on prayer. To the students, I'm sure this sounds antique. But on the last day of school, I had some come to me with the most beautiful prayer. I said, 'Where did you get this ?' They said, 'We made it up just for you.' I thought, Something went through. All year I've told them, 'Whenever you have to make a decision, you'd better pray about it first to know if it's the right decision to make.' I just hugged them all. 🙶

Dennis Creedon

Dennis Creedon is a reading specialist in the Philadelphia, Pennsylvania, public school system. For the last six years, he has been on special assignment as Director of Education to the Philadelphia Opera Company, where he designed a program that enables students in grades five through twelve to view opera productions at no charge. Over forty thousand Philadelphia public-school students have attended the opera since he began. He also created the Sounds of Learning education program, an interdisciplinary curriculum that allows students to read and study operas before attending them. In 1997 the program received a Best Practice in Arts Education citation from the state of Pennsylvania. He has been teaching for fifteen years.

❝ I am learning disabled. When I was a child, the doctors thought I had a brain tumor or leukemia because they couldn't figure anything out. At one point, I was put into St. Christopher's Hospital for Children, where I was kept under observation. While I was there, they introduced me to arts therapy. I was just playing in the arts room, and I heard one therapist turn to another and say, 'He's gifted. Look what he's doing.' No one had ever said that about anything I'd done before. I latched on to those words and the concept of the arts as a place where I could fit in.

I'm really attracted to opera as an educational medium. Opera is not only the most integrated of the arts—it has voice, drama, literature, dance, and orchestra—it's always been one of the most censored. The artist could communicate at different levels with the audience and take them to levels of thinking that at times threatened the political structure.

I was not an opera fan as a kid. I thought they were a bunch of fat, screaming people. I was sixteen when I got hired as an usher at the Academy of Music in Philadelphia. My father was jealous, because he listened to classical music, and I was getting paid to go there every night. My second year there, the head usher told me I was going into the opera. I said, 'I'm not into this.' He said, 'You will never forget it as long as you live.' He was a high-school teacher; I was in high school. He literally pulled me down the steps, seated me in the third row of the orchestra, and sat down next to me to make sure I wouldn't get up.

It was the beginning of the mad scene of *Lucia di Lammermoor*. The sets were unbelievable. The singer nailed it, to the point that I had electricity go up my spine. She was hitting the notes in a specific type of singing where you change your register extremely fast, so that she was the instrument above the orchestra. I couldn't believe that sound was coming out of her mouth.

After I went into public-school teaching, I wanted to take my kids to the opera, but the opera said no. I knew the opera. I worked for them; I poured their champagne. So I basically said, 'Come on, I won't embarrass you. They'll be well-behaved.' So the opera let them come in. It was for *Madame Butterfly*, and at the time, the development director studied my kids. She sat on the other side of the theater and watched them. At the end, when my girls cried and my boys were somberly silent, she couldn't believe it. She called me and said, 'Would you mind coming in with your lesson plans and explaining what you've done?'

The part I find most exciting as a teacher is that there are so many ways you can pull things in. For instance, in the curriculum for *Aida*, we have a lesson on interracial couples because the opera has one. There's also a war in *Aida*, so we have a lesson on violence, and then we talk about being safe at home or in the streets. We use the opera directly as a means of cracking content so that kids can talk about it in an informed way.

Our whole human essence is artistic. There was a situation where we had the kids in for a last dress rehearsal, and one of the artistic administrators was very upset because the children were whispering. 'There should be silence!' she said. And I said, 'They're not talking about the Phillies game or about the weather. They're talking about the opera. This is how they digest content. They have to share. They're going to tell us when it doesn't work.' And they did. In *Salome*, we had one of the guys commit suicide. He died too melodramatically, and the kids laughed. That was changed right after the last dress rehearsal.

We had seniors and juniors from high school see *Salome*, and the school superintendent was sitting with the kids. At one point Salome makes out with this decapitated head. It was dripping blood down her arms and legs, and all over the theater you had kids under their coats saying, 'Oh my god! I can't believe she's kissing that head!' I was in the balcony, and they were flipping out. I wish I'd had a camera.

The arts are a mechanism we can use with children to help them never forget who they are. Having been born learning disabled, the way I made it into the mainstream was through the arts. I want to insure that wherever children may be, they can latch on to curriculum that helps them find their own creative potential.”

Josephine Isabel-Jones, M.D.

Dr. Josephine Isabel-Jones is a professor of pediatrics (specializing in cardiology) at the UCLA School of Medicine in Los Angeles, California. She has been a teaching physician at UCLA for twenty-nine years.

❝ I decided to become a pediatrician from the age of eight. We had an old family doctor who was very kind and made us feel well. My mother's a teacher, and the positive image she showed me ultimately shaped my career. The excitement of learning spills over into wanting to teach, wanting to share that new knowledge. It makes it more exciting not just to have it but to be able to pass it on. If you don't have that attitude about passing it on, then I'm not sure you're going to be a very effective teacher. I know some excellent physicians who would be uncomfortable as teachers.

One of the things I try to have students understand is the effect that we as doctors might have on an individual or a family. With that in mind, you can present almost anything to a patient. If it's painful, you try to help them to work through it. It requires a sensitivity to look at whatever you're saying or doing and to say, 'Okay, how would I respond if I were in that position?' Most people appreciate when you're trying to be sensitive to their needs.

A lot of what we do in pediatric cardiology is pretty serious. It's not just your cold or a cut or bruise. Some of the problems you deal with are life-threatening. I had the good fortune of not having to learn by trial and error, but by observing how my mentors approached situations. I think we tend to become anxious if we know we're dealing with a life-threatening problem. But, again, we have to be sensitive to how we help the family.

I like my students to hurt a little bit. *I* hurt a little bit when we have patients whom we lose. It's important to acknowledge those feelings. I can remember a time when I would rather just make the announcement of bad news and move away, because I needed to protect myself. But then I learned that I needed to express the pain and help the family deal with it. It's important to let students know that. I've cried for patients that I've lost. And even knowing, anticipating that might happen, doesn't always take away the pain.

Being a good teacher is being a good student. Most knowledge, not just in medicine, evolves—including technology and everything that helps us open our eyes to new ways of doing things. Part of good teaching is teaching students to realize that you have to continue to learn.

Rachel Guido deVries

Since 1984 Rachel Guido deVries has been a visiting poet at elementary, middle, and high schools throughout New York State, conducting three- to five-day residencies in up to thirty school districts a year. She also teaches at Syracuse University and has taught creative writing in migrant camps, nursing homes, community centers, and at a psychiatric facility for convicted felons. She has been teaching for over twenty years.

❝ I try to get kids to write about themselves, to find metaphors to describe their hearts, souls, minds, bodies, and emotions. I show them a way to make metaphors very quickly, kind of a learning tool. I usually ask them to write something to do with a concept, like freedom, or what they wonder about, what they wish for, what they would do if they could re-create the world. A friend of mine who's a poet and essay writer has said in one of her books that poetry should be like a bowl. In it you put everything you need or wish for or want. I think that's a great metaphor for the usefulness, in fact, of all art. It allows the expression of feelings and ideas and beliefs that otherwise don't usually find a place in the regular school curriculum.

Usually the kids who don't like poetry say they don't like it because it's boring. I've gotten lots of kids to talk about how they think poetry's a girl thing, and to discover the ludicrousness of that notion. I've had some great conversations with kids of both sexes along the lines of, 'Well, where do you get the idea that poetry is boring? How can poetry all by itself be boring?' We talk, and I'll usually follow up with, 'What kind of music do you listen to?' Ninety-nine percent of the time the kids who don't like poetry will like rap music, which is perfect. Once we start talking about how rap is poetry, I'll say, 'What you mean is you don't like *some* poetry.' Most of it is stereotypes. By about fifth grade you see kids already having internalized this notion that poetry is boring. I tell them, 'If you don't like boring poetry, don't write any.'

I prefer teaching in alternative settings for a number of reasons. There's just no comparison to teaching a workshop to men and women who have been digging potatoes and are exhausted and refuse to come to the workshop until they've showered and cleaned up. Oftentimes it would be 9:00 or 10:00 at night before the workshop would start. These people had worked all day but still wanted to try writing poems and listen to me read them. In many ways, and the same is true of the prisoners [at the psychiatric facility], it made me come head to head with my own stereotypes and fears and broadened my understanding of how people are. Part of what I feel I do through poetry is hold up a mirror to whomever it is I'm working with and say, 'Look in, and reflect yourself. How do you want to be perceived?' That's what you can do in writing. And I think when you give people the opportunity to create themselves without holding them to what they've been, something wonderful happens.

I really think that for all kids, poetry is alternative education. I'm inviting them to write about things I know they don't get an opportunity to write about. So when they write about freedom, they incorporate talk about racism, and that leads to conversations about how race can factor in, whether it's a suburban school or in the middle of the city. This is one of the important things that poets can do. We have, I feel, a responsibility to give kids the opportunity to think about these issues.

The two issues that I'm always thinking about are identity and community. In the city, you find a very different community and identity. For one thing, the African-American community knows poets. I was at a friend's house, and there was a young African-American boy there, who at the time was in fourth grade. I mentioned something about Langston Hughes, and I had a book of black poets with me specifically for children, and this kid jumped out of his seat and said, 'Langston Hughes? That's my favorite poet!' and began reciting one of his poems. He performed it for me with all these gestures, pointing to his eyes, pointing to this, to that, and he said again, "That's my favorite poet!"

The central issue is, how do we get kids turned on to their own minds? At any level, the best poems are sometimes written by kids who are learning disabled or in the resource rooms. Teachers will come up to me and say, 'You know, if you had asked me who would do great, I would never have picked this kid or that kid.' That happens every year. So what poetry really is, I think, is the common language—because it's the language of truth, imaginatively and emotionally. It's not the language of reality. It's not about two plus two is four. It's about 'Like, two is cool, man.' It's about saying that two plus two is seventy-three. If it doesn't happen on planet Earth, then go play.

And when you play with language, I think you wake up to learning. Because then language becomes useful and pleasurable. It really incites a desire for true literacy. You write what you see, what you perceive, and what you feel. And I say this to kids all the time. You tell the truth with your heart, your feelings, and your mind, your imagination. That's what real feelings, real truths are like. All I'm doing is giving people permission to speak their truths, not what they've been told to believe. And when you do that, you'll find, for the most part, that we're pretty decent human beings.

If you want to write about a polka-dotted elephant for some reason, go ahead. If you're in a science class about the elephant and you write that the elephant has polka dots, that's a different story, but inside the poem, create the world you want to live in. That's my message, over and over again. Create the world you want to live in. 🙶🙶

Katie Sullivan

Katie Sullivan teaches third and fourth grade in a multiage classroom setting at the Warren Elementary School in Warren, Vermont. She also teaches a number of outdoor sports, including skydiving. She has been teaching for fourteen years.

66 I think there's a huge connection between why I teach and how I reconcile my doubts about teaching. I often think, 'I'm an impostor! I'm fooling people into thinking I know what I'm doing, and I don't.' Sometimes, if it gets so bad that I think maybe I shouldn't be teaching, I have an envelope with letters in it written by parents and colleagues and kids—anytime I get a positive letter from them, I put it in that envelope. I go back and read the letters, and then I say, 'I think I can keep doing this.'

The interesting difference between being an elementary teacher and being a high school or university teacher, I think, is that elementary schoolers are doing it all. Last year I built an indoor river in my classroom. It's just an amazing thing, and the kids love it. They did all the building. I had parents who came in—moms—who taught the kids how to use power tools. The river has a marsh at one end with all these wonderful marsh plants, and then the water flows down two waterfalls and gets pumped back into the marsh. It's just fabulous. And I'm so psyched that I'm in a school where I can have an indoor river. I've flooded the carpet twice!

I don't think teaching is boring, not one second of it, and I'm constantly changing what I do in order to find better ways of doing it. It's all kind of an adventure. To be able to make the river was a kind of scary undertaking, because I thought, What if I start and can't finish it? What if there's a huge disaster? What if everybody thinks it's ridiculous? And then I did it.

Trying to figure out each kid, every day, is such hard work. It's one of those things that people don't understand that teachers do. Again, it's sort of a twisted adventure. I'd say more of a daily challenge. The thing that makes teaching an adventure is the difficulty. It wouldn't be an adventure if it didn't have some kind of danger or uncertainty or risk. That's why as a teacher you never feel you've arrived, you never feel like you've figured it out, and you never feel like you're done. The school year is over in June, and you're like, 'Oh, I didn't do all of these.' And then you sort of have to say, 'Go forth. I hope you have a good life!'

So little of what we do as [elementary] teachers is teaching, you know. You're really just providing an environment for kids to do their own learning. The kids will do the learning if you make it a safe place for them. This year I'm going to get some people to make stilts for me, and all my kids are going to walk on stilts and be part of this wonderful show. Again, I'm thinking, What am I, crazy? But I always have to find something exciting to do. I need to be able to say, 'We're going to do long division, but we're also going to make stilts.' So there's a sense of adventure.

It's an interesting piece of my skydiving teaching, too. I spend a lot more time teaching skydiving than actually jumping. I'm on the ground in the classroom teaching people. But I just love teaching the first jump course and taking people on their first jump. Once they start getting more advanced, I lose interest in them as a skydiver. I teach to a level that if someone goes beyond me, they go beyond. Jumping out of a plane is not that hard for me. It's a really free thing, and wonderful and enjoyable to do. And I get to teach other people to do it and share that experience. I think there's a lot of correlation between how I feel teaching the first jump course and teaching about microorganisms in a river. The excitement is the same.

I don't think I would teach anything if I didn't get positive feedback. But the thing is, somebody being really excited about something *is* positive feedback. It doesn't have to be in the form of, 'You taught me that really well.' When someone does his or her first jump and lands on the ground and then comes running up to give you this huge hug, that's positive feedback. They're psyched about what they did, and sometimes they don't even remember that you played any part in it. But it's still feedback. ""

"I kind of take exception to the image of the teacher as a self-sacrificing man or woman. I get as much out of the experience as the kids do."

DIANE BUCHANAN
Language Arts Teacher
Norfolk, Virginia

Fulfillment

There can be a kind of fulfillment in teaching that few, if any, other professions offer. That's the overall view of the following teachers. Teaching makes a difference in their own lives as well as in the lives of their students. Their motivations for teaching are many, from ideas of service to feelings of happiness when students overcome limitations and succeed. All are motivated by the intrinsic rewards that teaching offers, rewards that have nothing to do with money. For these teachers, teaching fulfills their own needs as human beings to live complete and meaningful lives.

Shane McGregor

Shane McGregor is the director/instructor of Technology-in-Learning in Denver, Colorado. The organization focuses on teaching computer literacy and providing computer access for members of underserved communities. It includes after-school activities, computer clubs at local elementary and middle schools, and a youth development program at a local community center. It is funded by a public-service fellowship McGregor won from the Echoing Green Foundation. He has been teaching for two years.

❝ I started teaching after going through the computer-engineering program at Brown University. I'm the first one in my family to graduate from college, and I found statistics that only nine African-Americans had graduated with a computer-science degree from Brown in the last eight years. I said to myself, I'm going to take the skills I've learned and try to build a corps of young computer programmers by teaching them in middle school and high school. I had internships where I did the whole corporate thing, and financially they were very rewarding. But that wasn't what I wanted to do. I saw myself as having a bigger goal.

Most of the youth classes that I teach focus on how to develop World Wide Web pages for the Internet. I thought students could take advantage of this immediately, because the information displayed on the Internet is pretty much text- and graphics-based. You don't need a lot of technical skill to develop a Web page. Most students come in and want to play games initially. My whole focus is to steer them toward actually developing a game and learning the logical skills behind it. Being out of the school environment and having the freedom to do something creative and innovative really appeals to them.

It goes beyond teaching, I guess. It goes into the whole idea of mentorship and just being a friend, being able to say, 'You know, if you want to be involved with this, I'd be more than happy to help you.' The national statistics say that white families are three times as likely as blacks or Hispanics to have computers in their homes. Out of the students I work with, maybe 30 percent have computers, but they're all sort of that giveaway computer that was just lying around in somebody's house and got passed down. So they're not really useful. It's more immediate to have a washing machine than a computer.

I see my organization as developing into sort of a computer clubhouse at a local school—at different schools, actually. I've learned how to develop my curriculum pretty effectively for the people who are of high literacy, but also for those who have low literacy levels. I think a lot of volunteers can follow my curriculum and teaching materials pretty easily. I'm hoping to create a group of community computer consultants; it could even be some of the students I'm working with. They do feel a real sense of purpose in saying, 'I'm with this organization; I'm doing a Web page for such and such.'

I was very fortunate to win the scholarship to do what I'm doing. I had the opportunity either to make a lot of money or to do this and follow my passion. All the corporate interviews I went on afterward were just to get experience to teach the kids, 'Here's what they expect of you in an interview.' It's been a challenge for me to do all this teaching, because my family's not in the best financial situation. But knowing that there's a great good going on when I do go out there, and that I'm able to convey some type of wisdom to someone else, is all the reward that I could ever ask for. 🙶

Leonard Bruguier

Leonard Bruguier [Tahunska Tanka—Big Leggins] is an assistant professor of history at the University of South Dakota at Vermillion. He is also the director of the university's Institute of American Indian Studies and a member of the Yankton Sioux tribe. He has been teaching for eleven years.

❝ I was born on the Yankton Sioux reservation in 1944. My family cooked with wood and didn't have running water. Up until 1948 our major means of transportation was horse and wagon. After high school, I wanted to get out of South Dakota. The easiest way was to follow a long line of warriors in my family who'd served in the military. I joined the Marine Corps and knew I'd be earning benefits from the GI Bill. Unfortunately, Vietnam came up, and I served in a war zone. The reason I went into education is that I have a compelling need to serve, and to serve my people through education. It's also a way for me to pay back the people of this country for everything they've provided for me.

I teach because of the anticipation of being able to share my thoughts. I could never put a monetary value on the joy I see when students connect with thoughts—not necessarily mine—and decide that they're fully capable of thinking. Every now and then I get cards from my graduates, and they'll thank me or tell me they've found a wife or have a child, and they're finding their way in the world. That's what keeps me fired up.

As a professor, I can stand up there and machine-gun names, dates, times, and ideas. But my job is to take those kinds of facts and ideas and put them into a vision students can understand. For example, I feed birds, and this past year I built all my lectures about Siouan tribal culture on the idea of purple finches eating at my bird feeder. Bird and human patterns are mirror images. Babies cry, parents feed; you need only to observe traveling, feeding, and how they care for their young and elders to see that. Each bird is an individual, but it fits into a flock. It's fascinating to me.

My students understand that I'm a student, too. It opens a whole bunch of channels that would not exist if I did things in a different way. I'm not there to become popular, and they know that because I challenge them. But I don't push them too much. I've met certain qualifications and levels, but that doesn't mean I've quit learning. When I go down to the coffee shop and read a few poems I've written, it lets them know it's part of my job to create, too.

We have some very specific agendas as Indian nations, but we're also participating in this experiment called the United States of America, in terms of our military service and increasingly, I think, in higher education. I compare it to most immigrants who came to this country in masses, such as the Polish and the Italians. It took them two or three generations to get into the mainstream of corporate America. I'm thinking this is what's going to happen with the reservations. We are great survivalists. This country's policy was to exterminate us a hundred years ago, but they didn't; we're still here. We are the original inhabitants of this land. At some point, the country is going to recognize that and say, 'Hey, we need to make sure we keep the remnants of cultures that have been here for fifteen to twenty thousand years.'

I consider myself part of the spirit of the universe. I see us basically as human beings interacting with fellow human beings. In the process of learning these kinds of things, I've had to overcome being pulled into a position where I'm defending myself because of my race. The world is made up of a great diversity of races, and for me that's a beautiful thing.

I could be paid nothing and I'd still be teaching, simply because I consider myself one of the knowledge keepers of this world, and to me it's an obligation and a responsibility. I have this obligation and responsibility to the upcoming generation.

Keith Spence

Keith Spence is a guidance counselor at Clay Hill Elementary School outside of Jacksonville, Florida. He previously taught high-school math and computer science for nine years. He has been in education for eighteen years.

❝ When I first started as a guidance counselor, people said to me, 'I can see why you need one in high school, but why in elementary school?' A lot of it has to do with today's lifestyle. When I was growing up, I knew one kid whose parents were divorced. I remember talking to my parents about it. Their attitude was, You will never have to worry about that because we're a good family. So how do you think I felt down the road when I got divorced? People are moving around a lot more than they used to; neighborhoods are being torn up all the time. The world in which we live is a very different place than it was thirty years ago.

I'm a product of private schools, and have taught mostly in them. Before I took this job at Clay Hill, which is a public school, I called one of my teaching friends I'd kept in touch with over the years. I said, 'Is this something I can do?' She said, 'This is something that you need to do.' She felt I would be a better person and a better educator. 'You have blinders on,' she said. 'You need to see how the other half lives.'

I don't know if it's made me a better person. I came into a new family about the same time, so my role in life has been very different. In the summer of 1992, I got remarried, and my wife and her kids and I moved to the other side of Jacksonville. My whole life changed. I'd been a bachelor for ten years with a dog I came home to every night. Two weeks after we returned from our honeymoon, my dog died. Suddenly I had kids and a wife. So maybe I have more understanding now.

Working with kids is certainly fulfilling to me. Sometimes they'll open up and tell me things they won't tell the principal. I like working one-on-one. I like being able to talk to kids on the sidewalk. I like seeing improvement, and dealing with kids over a period of time and seeing how they change. Guidance is part of the helping profession, whether it's counseling I've lined up or a Thanksgiving basket I've been able to get together for a family. I've always wanted to be in a position where I'm helping others. I feel I do that more when I work individually with kids. If a student can attend one more year of school or go on to graduate from high school or even attend college, then I've been successful.

Our society is becoming more technological. We really need better-educated people. There's an old adage, 'If you teach a person to fish, he can feed himself for life.' It's teaching people to be successful—I think there's a certain joy in that. We want our own kids to have a better life than we had. I guess I look at the bigger picture in our school system and at how so many of our families are from low socioeconomic backgrounds. A major reason is a lack of education. So if I can help one person or a group of people to enjoy learning, they will do better for themselves; that, in turn, will do more for our society.

A teacher I worked with a couple of years ago said she looks at every one of her students as a potential neighbor. She said, 'Is he going to be a good parent? Is he going to raise a good family? How can I help him now so that he will be a good neighbor ten years down the road?' Sometimes we succeed. And the times that we do are wonderful. 99

Karen Saupe

Karen Saupe is an associate professor of English at Calvin College, the college of the Christian Reformed Church in Grand Rapids, Michigan. She has also taught high-school English. She has been teaching for fourteen years.

❝ One of my favorite courses to teach is Shakespeare. Every play addresses my students directly, and it's such a wonderful thing for them to discover. After a few weeks of being uncomfortable with the language and thinking they're looking at something faraway and weird, they suddenly realize they have all sorts of intimate connections with that world, and really what my students are learning about is themselves and the other people in their world. It's got nothing to do with anything that happened in the fourteenth or sixteenth century. It's about them.

While I was in graduate school at the University of Rochester, I worked as a study-skills counselor. I would ask kids, 'What's your major?' and they'd say, 'Pre-med,' and I'd say, 'Why?' They'd say, 'I want to be a doctor,' and I'd say, 'Why?' and they'd say, 'Well, um, my parents want me to be a doctor' or 'I want to be successful.' I had a fair number of kids who really didn't have any love of the thing they were studying, and more than a few to whom I'd say, 'If you could do anything you wanted, what would you do?'

If you ask Calvin students when they're freshmen what they want to major in, they'll often say, 'I'm waiting to discover what God wants me to be.' To me, that's very healthy and important. The goal at Calvin is to integrate faith and learning, not to set one aside in favor of the other. And I don't think faith is solely the property of a religious institution. I wish every kid who went into college could say, 'I'm waiting to discover what I'm going to become; I'm waiting to find out what I'm interested in.'

I had a student about a month ago who, in an intro-to-lit class for nonmajors—the lowest common denominator for a literature class at Calvin—failed his second test and was suddenly deeply, deeply worried, and interested. I thought, What's the occasion? This was a kid who had sat in back with his baseball cap pulled down over his eyes for the whole semester despite repeated invitations to sit someplace where he could hear, and I knew he was on the verge of flunking out. I said, 'Come to my office. I'm going to yell at you awhile, and then I'm going to help you.' He said okay.

I said, 'Why do you even care about this class?' And he said, 'Because I want to stay at Calvin.' I said, 'Doesn't it make you mad to have to take classes that have no bearing on your life?' And he said, 'What?' I said, 'If this doesn't matter to you, if you can't see a relationship between these poetry terms I'm trying to make you memorize and your own life, then they have no meaning and this is a waste of your money.' Then I asked, 'What do you want to do when you grow up?' He said, 'I'm going to be a building contractor like my dad.' I said, 'Why? What interests you?' He started talking about building houses and putting them together and creating. Then I started talking about poetry and poets' choices and the poets' tools and how literary devices and figurative language fit in. Once I could make him see a relationship, he was willing to go think about it.

So I gave him another chance to raise his grade by watching TV and coming up with twenty examples of figurative language, or some dumb thing like that. He came back a week later with a long list. I said, 'Did you learn anything?' He said, 'Sure.' I said, 'Like what?' He said, 'Well, it was kind of fun.' And I said, 'Okay. That's all I want to know.' Because you learn things when it's a pleasure to learn them.

I consider it a good day or week when I've learned something about Shakespeare, or whatever I'm teaching, from a student who doesn't even realize that what he or she is saying is brilliant. I had a lot of idealistic reasons for going into teaching that I put on my teaching applications and that I believed—and still do—but the bottom line is that I find it gratifying to be in a classroom. When I was little, one of the things I thought I wanted to be was an entertainer of some kind. Well, I am. There's a lot of public relations here. There's a lot of entertaining, sometimes acting, a lot of persuading, arguing, studying, research. It's almost as if every other career you could possibly want gets to be part of the picture here.

I started out thinking that if I ever found something I'd rather do, I would go do it, because as a student, I had teachers who were tired, bored, and disliked us; I also had teachers who loved us. Both of those kinds of teachers made me want to teach. There's a retired man at Calvin who apparently taught every course the English Department offered during his career. And I think, What a wonderful goal! I'll probably never do that; I don't think you can anymore. But right now I just want to teach the same three courses fifty times until I get them right—and then try something new. 💬

Rose Steiner

Rose Steiner teaches math at an adult education center within the Billings, Montana, school district. She has been teaching for over twenty years.

66 I reach out to struggling students. I take great satisfaction in seeing accomplishments made by students who think they're so dumb they'll never learn math. The students I get in adult ed usually admit that they're struggling with math more than they'll admit they're struggling with writing. It hits them in the face. 'I can't do it,' they say. 'I'll never understand.' I reach out to those students by backing up and finding out, Where is it that they lose their understanding?

Since I started in the school district, I've been teaching an open-entry/open-exit class. It's five classes, actually. I might have 130 to 150 students that I'm working with at any one time, but they're not coming every day, and you don't know when they're coming. My classes will be totally mixed. Students sign up to come for an hour on maybe Monday, Wednesday, and Friday. I have a different group almost every hour, and very few students stay more than an hour. So it's chaotic in some ways, because you're jumping from working on adding numbers and lining up place values to a question on adding polynomial equations.

You have to be aware of where your students are and start from there to try to help them. In adult ed, a lot of the students have come to the point where they know they want to learn. We're kind of tied in with a college, and if a student doesn't have a good pretest in math, it's suggested that he or she come down to our program. I've had students come who are scared or frustrated or afraid of math, and they've ended up leaving my classroom saying, 'I can even see majoring in that!'

What I find is that because I'm working with all the levels, I see interconnections among the math concepts. It's really easy for me to build understanding for my students because I'm constantly reinforcing these ties. There are patterns of things that are the same throughout math. As the student starts seeing the pattern, all the things start fitting together. Otherwise, if you have all these rules, and you don't know which rule to use when, it gets scary.

I think what keeps me teaching is the reward of being able to help someone. There are so many students who have been frustrated trying to pick up things in education. I've always had the willingness to work with a student. I've given them my home phone number and told them to call if they have problems—I can work with them over the phone. I've done that many times. We need teachers who are willing to do that instead of just standing at the front of the classroom and saying, 'Now you guys have got it, so see you tomorrow.'

I feel like my whole reason to be living is sharing what I can so that someone else can improve. I'm always trying to find a better way to teach my students. I've been able to take each one and find out where they are. They are in need of someone caring about them. That's a big part of my teaching—to let the student know that if no one else is, I'm here for them.

Diane Buchanan

Diane Buchanan teaches eighth-grade language arts and reading at Thomas Eaton Middle School in Hampton, Virginia. She is also an adjunct instructor in the Darden College of Education at Old Dominion University in Norfolk, Virginia. She has been teaching for sixteen years.

❝ I don't see teaching as something you 'do' to kids. I don't see it as, you have all this knowledge and they don't, and they come to you with this deficit, and your role is to fill it. When kids come to me, they come with a whole set of prejudices and things they know. They're not deficient in any sense, nor am I the answer. I'm just as deficient in my own ways as they are. So I feel that their education is something that gets negotiated. Part of it is that I have to make them want it, and the other part is that we have to do it so that it's not just my way. It's something we have to construct together.

My classroom has to be a community of learners. I set up the parameters, of course, because ultimately I'm responsible. I know there are certain things they need to be able to do by the time they leave me as literate eighth-graders. There should be certain ways that they can read and write, communicate and think, but I have to make them value those. I can't force them to value what I'm giving them. We need to enter into a relationship. I feel that my kids know me very well; they know who I am and what I'm about. I only ask them to do what I myself do. If I ask them to keep a writer's notebook, I keep one, too. If I ask them to read something, I read it also. If I ask them to discuss openly, they have the right to expect me to do the same. In my classroom we're in this together. Quality is never an issue, and neither is rigor. I expect them to be honest, to work hard, and to value what they do. If they don't, who will?

Along the way I hope they figure out who they are. I think that what I do has a direct connection to who they are. I want my kids to understand that they can discover what's inside of them through their reading, writing, speaking, and listening. They don't have to be like everybody around them; they don't have to buy into that unless they want to. Hopefully, when they leave me, they are a little brighter and a little smarter about themselves.

I expect them to pay attention to the life they have. My bright kids freak out. 'Just tell me what to write,' they say. 'Just tell me how many paragraphs, how many words; I'll write whatever you want.' I'm sure they could. But when you ask them to tell you what's important, or if they liked a book, they say, 'Yeah it was good.' Well, why was it good? 'It was interesting.' Why?

I kind of take exception to the image of a teacher as a self-sacrificing woman or man. I get as much out of the experience as the kids do. They keep me thinking; I'm never bored. I'm different today than I was a year ago, and that's because of the kids I've come in contact with.

I try to go in as a decent human being and show them what it's like to be one. I try not to bully them. I try to develop in them a sense of right from wrong, a sense of ethics. We groan and complain about kids today. Well, they're here because we had them. They didn't spring fully formed! Some of us out there are truly lousy parents. I'm a parent, and I'm sure I've had some lousy moments. But I feel like teaching is what I do well. I don't mean that in arrogance. I think that it's my gift to give back. I think that you can teach a kid to think, to ask questions, to look around, and to wonder. I'm not even interested in the answers, but in keeping them asking questions. To me, there is so much power there.

I don't think you should teach unless it's a conscious choice. You hear people say, 'Those who can, do, and those who can't, teach.' I'm sorry, but I don't think you'd last one day if you were not meant to teach. I don't think you're ever going to do it perfectly. I used to work at a bank, and I knew that if my window balanced, I'd had a perfect day. If you're looking for that kind of a job, this isn't it. The satisfaction has to come from within. You have to be self-sustaining. You have to be content to not always have the answers. You have to be willing to give it your all and not hold back. 💬💬

Lee Beall

Lee Beall is a special music consultant and teacher for the Winston-Salem/Forsyth County schools in Winston-Salem, North Carolina. He specializes in music for preschool children and children with special needs. In 1994 he retired as a professor of music from Winston-Salem State University. He has been teaching for over forty years.

❝ I came to Winston-Salem around 1970. My wife is also a teacher, and I went to her school to visit. There was a class of mentally handicapped, trainable students who had IQs from fifteen to fifty. She said, 'These children don't get music because the law doesn't allow it.' At that time I thought, If typical children could benefit from music, then why couldn't atypical children? I asked the school system if I could volunteer my time, which they allowed me to do. I worked with the children for a year or two. Then I thought, If typical high-school students can put on a musical at the end of the school year, why can't we?

The first thing that came to mind was *Oliver*. My wife happened to be studying it with her fifth-grade students; at the time, my students were ages sixteen to twenty-one, and they were housed in the grades-five-and-six school. My wife wrote the script, and we involved all the children in the school. There was a class of hearing-impaired students, and they participated. Actually, [the role of] Oliver was played by a hearing-impaired student. We had another child be a translator on the stage. The next thing we did was *Oklahoma*. I got permission from the Rogers and Hammerstein library to rewrite it for my atypical students.

When you see a production of ours, you know that the music isn't the end. It's getting the children together or getting them up on stage. You see children on crutches and with leg braces off moving and dancing in their own way, and then you understand. It's about acceptance and what you can do, and trying to make that better, and then being happy with yourself. That's what I aim at. The students have been told they're wrong so many times. I don't need to tell them anymore. When the kids are proud of what they can do and not afraid to stand up and say, 'Here I am and this is my music,' to me that's the beautiful part of it.

I make the statement that my children sing in harmony all the time; that means, of course, that just as they're developmentally delayed in many aspects, they're delayed in music, and often they don't get their pitches correct— but it doesn't matter because we know they are in the process of becoming themselves. One day they might sing on pitch. Many of my students do now. I also teach in a preschool handicapped program, and it is almost becoming typical that we have children sing first who have never spoken. Then they start to speak. We know we can teach children through music.

When I work with the younger children, I make a joke with the principal. I say, 'As soon as I get these children to sing on pitch, you move them out into a typical school.' When my high-school students start singing on pitch, what will that mean? That they can sing in the church choir, which will give them an outlet after they get out of school. We just accept whatever we can get from the kids. At least it's a beginning.

I do this because I want the children to succeed. That's my joy. I try to get beautiful sounds from them, but if I don't get the beautiful sounds, I don't make them sit down. It's like a church choir. When do you tell a lady who has sung in the choir for eighty years that it's time to stop? Is there a time? I'd say no. For me there is just never a time when you tell a person that he or she can't do something. You believe—that's how you teach your own children.

The importance is not in the beauty of the sound but in the fact that somebody is doing it. They will learn to sing on pitch, maybe not by the time they're twenty-one, but maybe later on. Plenty of mine do. The joy is in seeing them succeed, seeing them perform, seeing them do what they can. When they succeed it means that I've succeeded, and that makes me happy. 99

"I love what I'm doing. I love the idea that I can impact someone else's life."

NICHOLAS KAMARAS
History Professor
Pemberton, New Jersey

Love

Is it possible to love your job? According to the following teachers, the answer is yes. These teachers are passionate about what they do and why they do it. Some of them feel a kinship with their students, whether the students are children or adults. Others are in love with the idea of education and the opportunities it offers for self-discovery and growth. *Love* can mean many things, but for these teachers it expresses how engaging and stimulating their work is, and how positive they feel about their experiences, their students, and themselves.

Tracy Heinrich

Tracy Heinrich teaches first and second grade in a mixed-age class at Irvington Elementary School in Portland, Oregon. She has been teaching for ten years.

❝ I sit in front of my class, and I look at them and think, I love what I do. It's hard to explain more than that. I was out of the classroom for two years, and I never felt that way. I was never able to say, 'I love my job.' When I got back and I could look at these kids, look at their faces and see the interest and excitement they hold for learning, that just excited me.

I remember probably four or five years ago, a kid wrote me a letter. It was after the second day of school. What he wrote was, 'The first day of school was like biting into a chocolate pie.' I thought that was the ultimate compliment. Me and chocolate, we go hand-in-hand! I had that on my bulletin board the entire year. It's those little, tiny things that make the difference.

I had a parent last year who wrote me the most incredible letter. I've had wonderful relationships with parents and ended up making friends with a lot of them. I'm holding this letter and thinking, 'This is why I do this, because I've made a difference in her child's life.' Being a parent myself, I know how important that is, to have somebody else take the time to care about my child. That's amazing to me.

When I get into the classroom, I don't think about the stuff that's going on outside of it. I'm focused on my kids and what we're doing. I could be in the worst mood in the morning, after fighting with my kids, trying to get them dressed, and getting them off to school and to day care. Then I walk into class and I'm just so happy to see my students. I still don't quite understand how that works. It happens.

Some days the results of teaching are negative. I'm not happy and the kids aren't happy. It seems like a waste. I try to make sure that doesn't happen very often, because I think it's important that every kid strives to feel positive every day. If kids have a teacher who's negative or who's not happy about being there, it reflects on the kids. They pick up every little thing. Kids are pretty smart.

This is not an easy job. I know that years ago, this was what girls did when they didn't know what they wanted to do. When I got out of high school, I didn't know. But if you don't want to work hard, then you'd better get out of teaching. If you think it's an easy September-to-June job, you are in for a huge surprise. I've been in a lot of different jobs, and teaching is definitely the most stressful, because it deals with children's lives.

I believe in what I'm doing. I'm pretty passionate about my work. I think that's an important part of it. I do get discouraged some days. You have those days. It's not all fun and games. It's difficult to put into words why it is that I get up every morning and go to my job, except that it's something I enjoy. I can't imagine doing anything else at this point in my life. 🙷🙷

Barbara Renoux

Barbara Renoux teaches third grade at Ipalook Elementary School in Barrow, Alaska. In 1996 she was selected as Alaska's State Teacher of the Year in conjunction with the U.S. Department of Education. She has been teaching for nineteen years.

What keeps me teaching is that I can be as creative as I want. Things are never boring or stagnant. There's something that happens almost every day that makes me laugh or cry, or that I write in my journal. I either sit back and say, 'That lesson went well' or 'That lesson was horrible! I've got to start all over and do something different.' I love that feeling.

Barrow is as far north as you can go in the United States. It's solid tundra. There are no trees. For a few months in the summer, you'll get patches of green and flowers, but it's very wet. It gets to about fifty degrees below zero in the winter. If you dress warmly, it's not a big deal. We wear T-shirts in our homes and schools; it's very warm in the buildings. Getting to and from the buildings is the tricky part.

My students are mostly Eskimo. All the teachers come up from the lower forty-eight [states]. Eskimo culture is really different. Eskimos are into hunting, sustenance fishing, and whaling. Whaling is a big part of their culture. In the fall and in the spring, you'll see them bring huge bullhead whales up on the beach; the whole village comes out to celebrate the harvest. They cut open the whales and share them. It's totally different from anything I've ever experienced.

Traditional reading, writing, and arithmetic education is not always valued the same way it is in the lower forty-eight. Eskimo adults feel it's more important for their children to learn their culture and the things they do to survive on the tundra. The students have an Iñupiat teacher whom they see forty-five minutes every day, so the culture is kept alive through these classes. [Iñupiat refers to the language and culture of the native group in northern-most Alaska, Canada, and Siberia.] Their native language is Iñupiat, and it's mostly the older generation that speaks it fluently. Sadly, it's a dying language. Even though they teach it in the schools, it hasn't really caught on to where the kids speak it fluently. We get together with the Iñupiat teachers, and sometimes they're able to blend what we do in our classrooms with the culture they're teaching in theirs. For the kids, it's like they have one foot in that culture and the other in English culture. In the meantime, the English ends up to be what we call 'village English.' They leave out a lot of words such as conjunctions, so it's a difficult thing to teach reading and writing. Their speaking and communication skills are not really English and not really Iñupiat.

Sometimes if we're reading stories and there's humor, or double meanings or puns, they don't get them. I remember the first time I said, 'Wake up and smell the coffee!' to a student. They all looked at me like I was crazy. I tried to explain how sometimes we say silly things. Then they waited for me to say it again. Every now and then, they'll say, 'Wake up and smell the coffee!' and start laughing hysterically, as if it's the funniest thing they've ever heard.

It can be a challenge trying to teach the differences among the four seasons, too. Barrow doesn't have four seasons. The students don't know what spring or fall is. I remember talking to them once about pumpkins during Halloween. They know what pumpkins are because we have them shipped up from Anchorage. I asked my mom, who lives in Wisconsin, to go to a pumpkin patch and take a video. She sent the tape up to me. She also taped some apple trees in an orchard. I was showing the kids the video, and the first thing that came on was the apples. They were so amazed to see that apples come from trees and not just from the grocery store. We stopped at that point and talked about trees. I said, 'The next part you're going to see is the pumpkins.' One little boy said, 'I can't wait to see what the pumpkin tree looks like!' They really have no idea about things we take for granted.

I don't think teaching is a profession about which you can say, 'Maybe if I work harder, it'll come easier.' There's got to be a connection, some sort of spark or electricity that says it's right for you. We started school last week, and I said to my students, 'Out of all the professions, I can't think of anything I'd like to do more than be a teacher.' I remember thinking as a kid, Tomorrow is the first day of school. I can't wait! After eighteen years, I still get that feeling. 🟈🟈

Shirley Neighbors

Shirley Neighbors teaches biology, anatomy, and physiology at Career High School in New Haven, Connecticut. She has been teaching for thirty years.

❝ My students love—at least they tell me they love—my style of teaching. I never sit. I'm all over the place, up this row, down that row, really getting a feel for them quickly. We have mutual respect in the classroom. That's all I teach about on day one. I give them my guidelines for success for the year. It's twenty-six statements they keep in their notebooks. They include rules about clothing (whether they can wear hats, which is no) and profanity (which is no), the kinds of notebooks they need to keep and when they're going to be collected, how often we'll have a quiz or a test, etc. The students love those guidelines because I make them a sure thing. I don't want a student to come in two or three minutes late on day two and say, 'You didn't say anything to me yesterday about this.' I tell them, 'When you come in here, I want you to pay attention.'

I've had kids tell me, 'I always feel safe when I come into your room, because I know you're not going to allow someone to start name-calling and nit-picking and just really making me have a lousy day.' I can count on one hand the number of students that I send out a year for discipline. Usually I'll have fingers left. I think it's the way I try to handle discipline problems that makes a difference. Are you trying to embarrass the student, or to find out why that student is constantly late for your class? I try to be fair—tough, but fair. And I try to observe a lot.

New Haven is a great place to teach. As a city it offers a lot, not only for students, but for teachers. When you talk about inner-city kids, sometimes you think that perhaps the high schools are inferior because they're overshadowed by violence or whatever else happens. Career High School is a magnet school; students apply, and we're on a lottery system. We have a collaboration with Yale that I helped develop in 1993 to prove that inner-city students can learn anatomy on a sophisticated basis. The students work with human cadavers. It's taught by first- and second-year medical students and some of the professors. We've had a good response: grades have gone up, as well as interest in anatomy/physiology. Ninety percent of the students who have completed the course are in college right now. It's a bimonthly lab over at Yale, and the kids are usually on the bus before I am. They work very hard.

The number-one reason I teach is commitment, and love of the profession. If you feel you have something within you that can truly make a difference in the lives of kids, then that's why you do it. I want to make sure that kids don't fall along the wayside. I think that's my special calling. I know it meant a lot in high school having teachers interested in me, cushioning me, telling me I could do things. I try to impart that to the students I work with.

I'm there to serve them. I may not be able to help everyone, but I've got to lead them in the direction where they can get the help they need. I try to find whatever it is I can do to make a difference. That's basically what teaching is all about. You try to touch their lives and to make sure it's a positive touch. 🙄🙄

Linda Dehnad

Linda Dehnad has taught English as a Second Language at Kansai Gaidai Hawaii College in Honolulu, Hawaii. She recently began teaching French at Le Jardin Academy, an independent school in Kailua, Hawaii. She has been teaching for over ten years.

I used to sell real estate in California to support my family. I became a smashing real-estate agent. I always felt like I was running a one-room schoolhouse, because people came in and needed to be educated about the housing market and buying a house. I had people at all stages, from beginner to advanced. People liked what I did, because when they talked, I could figure out what they were trying to say that they weren't sure of in their own minds. And that's what teaching is: listening to people and hearing the messages behind the words. When people are buying or selling a house, they're usually at a crisis point. They're shaken, and they need somebody to make them feel that it's okay.

To be a teacher, you have to live in the world of ideas. If you're going to make anybody else excited about that world, you have to find out where the point of romance in learning is in them, and connect with it. You really have to be involved intellectually in what you're doing; you can't do it mechanically. When I go into a classroom, the outside world disappears. If I'm nervous, I love to go and teach. I'm not nervous about anything while I'm teaching.

The first word that comes to mind about why I teach is *love,* in the human or universal sense. I'm excited about ideas. Sometimes I cry when the students write something that's beautiful. There's hardly anything else that moves me that way. I think that teaching's my art. For a while I painted. Sometimes I write and translate poetry. But I feel like my class is where I'm most creative. I help people to want to be there. And when they know you love them, they love you back, too.

I think it's a little political to teach this way, because you have to be comfortable with truth and freedom of ideas. There was a guy—the greatest traditionalist in our department—who once said to me, 'You're my worst nightmare.' I walked by his classroom and heard him teaching and realized that he absolutely loves the students as much as I do. So I don't think I have the corner on the market.

You have to do anything you can that makes you alive intellectually, such as reading literature. You have to show students that your mind is working. That's the only thing that's really interesting to them. They don't like questions with answers. They like questions without answers. Ask them a question to which you don't know the answer. Those are the ones they want to know about. 🙶🙶

Edith Rivera

*Edith Rivera teaches eighth- and ninth-grade English at
Rafael Martinez Naddal Intermediate School in Guaynabo,
Puerto Rico. She has been teaching for twenty-six years.*

❝ Puerto Rico is a commonwealth of the United States.
That means we have the same currency, a lot of similar
laws, and our own constitution based on the Constitution
of the United States. Puerto Ricans are American citizens
and serve in the Armed Forces; the only thing we don't do
is vote for president. We are mostly a Spanish-speaking
country. We're not fully bilingual, but many people understand English. We have a lot of the United States over here,
only in a tropical way.

I have students who migrate constantly. Their parents
go to New York and stay maybe six months, then they
come back. I can really empathize because I went through
the same thing. I was raised in the States. My father was in
the army, so we traveled a lot. We lived in Germany, but
mostly I grew up near Chicago. When my father was dis-
charged we came back to Puerto Rico. I didn't want to
come back. It was hard for me to adjust in school; everything was so different. I had to go to a private school to get
used to the idea of speaking Spanish.

I teach in English. We group our students because we
have some who are advanced. Other students can't com-
pete, so I have to work with them on a remedial level.
Sometimes I have to reinforce with Spanish. The kids tend

to not really like English, so it's kind of an uphill battle. The Spanish teacher is constantly telling me, 'I don't know how you do it. I can't get them to read in Spanish, much less in English.' I have to be part actress, part singer, part everything to get them to digest what I'm trying to teach.

Ninety-five percent of our students are from low-income families. Some students live only with one parent; others live with a grandmother because their parents abandoned them. Of the one hundred fifty students I teach, if I get through to thirty, if I get through to ten, if I get through to five, that's what keeps me going. I see them in later years working in the local banks as tellers, or I see them in the supermarket. They say, 'Ah, Miss E.! I remember when we did this and this. I remember this.' And then you think, It really worked. You thought they didn't listen, but you see that you got to them.

Last week I did an activity with my homeroom. It was an exercise on how to improve relationships with each other. The feedback was great. We had a hugging session and talked about how a hug a day is really good. They came up and hugged me. I realized that most of them were really hungry for that. I thought, 'Whatever they don't get from me about English, they'll get somewhere else. The love, the attention, the listening are what's important.'

Every time I have a problem in the classroom, I just talk to the student. I say, 'What is it? What's wrong?' I take the time to listen. You wouldn't believe some of the things I hear. As teachers, I think sometimes we tend to miss that. We're so busy with, 'What is a noun? What is a verb? What is part of history?' that we forget there's a person inside. Many of them come from homes where they don't get a pat on the back or a hug. Many of them don't know how to reciprocate love, and you can tell. They're very arrogant, or they don't want you to come too close. But slowly, you start breaking all those barriers.

You need to look at a student as a person, not as a number in your row book. You need to see what makes the student tick, and try to find that personal part. Then maybe you can get to the educational part. I'm supposed to retire in five years, but I still have a lot more to give. As long as I enjoy teaching, I'm hanging in there. It's my country we're talking about, the future of Puerto Rico. Where are these kids going? Where is my country going? If all the teachers bail out, what's going to happen? I've had good experiences and bad experiences. Out of the bad you make good. That's what a smart teacher has to learn how to do.

It's up to us as teachers to educate our students. The more educated you are, the more you can accept changes, or the more you can see what's going on around you. It's not just listening to whoever has something to say, it's knowing what you think from your own experience. We have to educate. As long as there are teachers willing to do that, we will have an educated country, and an educated island whose people will know what they truly want. 🙶

Jean Gilbert

Jean Gilbert teaches second grade at La Mesa Elementary School in La Mesa, New Mexico. She spent ten years in special education before becoming an elementary teacher. She has been teaching for twenty-six years.

❝❝ Every morning when I go to class, it's what I want to do. I'm a person who has a lot of energy. And I really use it in the classroom!

I think about other professions or job options and what would I want to do if I weren't teaching. And I still find myself being in education. I've thought about humane education or environmental education. Children and animals are the loves of my life. I've thought about things like storytelling. I have a friend who's in a storytelling league, and I just love the work she does. It's exciting to think about what I could do on animal-rights ethics through storytelling, through music and drama. This may be another reason why I love teaching: because it's *me*. I bring in my outside interests all the time.

We recently did a unit on companion animals, so I brought in our dog. I'm involved with NAHABE [National Association for Humane and Bilingual Education]. They had a nationwide banner contest focusing on companion animals. Our class banner was chosen as the best in the state of New Mexico. It was about spaying and neutering. We did hand prints all over it, and we sewed on some sequins and stuff; a parent helped. I do this kind of thing all the time. Some things are determined more by what's happening at a given moment. We had baby turtles in our backyard, and I knew the kids would love them because we'd just done a unit on reptiles. I brought the turtles to school, and the kids drew pictures of them and wrote to their pen pals about them. We took the turtles outside. I also brought mealworms, because mealworms are like candy to turtles, and the kids got to feed them to the turtles.

I'm a vegetarian, and my perspective years ago was almost militant. I don't know if I conveyed that in the classroom; I suppose I did to a certain extent. But now I take a gentler approach. When we had our class cookout, I had a tofu hot dog, and the kids just couldn't believe it. They would have sworn I was eating meat! I had to show them the package. It is important just to live other choices, and not to imply there's only one choice anybody *has* to make.

When I brought my dog to school, we talked about how she's spayed, and why that's the best thing. A lot of these kids say their dogs have had puppies, and their dogs and cats have been run over. But I don't want children to feel burdened, because it isn't their responsibility. I guess I'm trying to offer more of a balanced way of looking at things, and to show them that there are choices rather than, 'This is the only way things are done.' 99

Nicholas Kamaras

Nicholas Kamaras teaches American history, Western civilization, and political science at the University of Southern Colorado, which has a campus on McGuire Air Force Base in New Jersey, and at Burlington County Community College in Pemberton, New Jersey. He has been teaching at the college level for twenty-seven years.

❝❝ Teaching is a performance. It's timing. You want to keep your students' attention. You don't want to give them all the conclusions at the beginning of class, and you don't want to give them all the conclusions at *any* time. I make it clear that I'm going to be straightforward and honest with them. I have two objectives: I don't want to bore my students, and I don't want to waste their time. So I try to inform them but at the same time stimulate them to think.

I had a young lady in a class who was convinced that Abraham Lincoln was a Democrat and that he had freed the slaves because the Democrats were the party of liberal policies. And nothing, even taking books and showing her, could explain the truth. Yet, she was curious, and after she sat down and thought about it and discussed it with her husband and family, she wanted to find out more.

I once had fifty and sixty students in classes. Sometimes you think, How do I make them ask questions? How do I make them respond? Well, if you handle it properly, you can. You can make them feel like a group of ten or twelve or fifteen. It's your approach. Some students say,

'Should I just put my Social Security number down on the test, or my name?' And I always tell them, 'Put your name,' because I respect them. They're there for a purpose, and I want to help them fulfill it. I respect them because they have something to offer not only to their own world, but to me. I can learn from them. And then I can take what I learn and turn it around and use it on my behalf.

I look forward to going to class. I look forward to presenting a specific lecture that I think my students can learn from and that can help shape their lives. I enjoy it when I hear from someone ten or fifteen years later, which happens all the time. Now they have children, or maybe they need help. They say, 'I don't even know if you remember me, but I'm in a jam, and I was wondering, can you help me?' That makes me feel so good, that I'm someone they felt they could call and get a genuine response from.

I love what I'm doing. I love the idea that I can impact someone else's life. It's not just the teaching of history or political science or Western civilization, it's the ability to help people deal with their own thoughts, not only in the classroom but outside of it. The other night I was waiting for someone in the parking lot, and one of my students was standing there in the rain. I said, 'Why are you in the rain? Are you waiting for a ride?' And she proceeded to tell me that she suffers from depression. She's on Prozac, and she really came to class to meet other people. But she's depressed all the time. Now we talk and she calls me once in a while. So it's not just in the classroom; it's the ability to help students in other ways.

About six years ago, I was teaching a young lady, and she sent me a Christmas card. She wrote a little note in the card and told me that when she was twelve years old, she was raped by her baby-sitter. She had never told anyone before. But I had talked to the class in general about being honest and forthright, not only with others but with yourself, and about trying to get help when you can. Once I got the letter from her, other things fell into place in terms of what she had said in class. Now she is getting help, and she feels as though a load has been lifted off her. I'll never forget that for the rest of my life. That makes me feel so good! That one young lady, who was maybe twenty-one or twenty-two, who had this horrible thing happen to her and lived with it for ten or eleven years, is maybe starting to come back—and that I, in a little way, contributed. 99

Gina Davis

For the last six years, Gina Davis has been an adult and correctional educator at the Sussex Correctional Institution in Georgetown, Delaware. She has also taught middle-school special education. She has been teaching for twenty years.

66 I never went into a prison until the first day I started work, not even to look before I made my decision. I've learned more about myself since then.

I started out working in prison with very small groups of handicapped eighteen- to twenty-one-year-olds. Most had trouble reading or trouble with math. I had hardly any with good academic skills; in fact, some were semi-retarded. We were looking at maybe fifteen students in that age group at the time, and maybe six who came regularly because they hadn't been out of school for too long. I taught them for about a year and a half. I went to three different buildings and taught in the chow halls. The beginning of the third year I was there, a math teacher in the adult high-school program retired, so I offered to teach any age-group. I found out that the older inmates were really good role models for my kids who were kind of flighty and ornery. I saw a transformation almost right away with the kids observing their behavior and fitting into it. At that point I asked some inmates to help me tutor.

I had three very different characters. I never expected that three people could have as much influence on my life as they have had, in a positive way, and in a rough way sometimes. Two of them had been in jail for over twenty years, and the third was on death row. He was black, and he had a very good rapport with the black inmates. He had a lot of patience, so he worked with a couple of lower-functioning younger men. Even though I knew he was on death row, I never considered that he would be executed. He had been in jail for about thirteen years. I went to the pardon board, which I'd never done before nor since, and spoke on his behalf, but he was executed.

I've found my assertiveness in this job. I'm not really assertive in other ways in my life. Before I got my teaching certification, I'd go to these job interviews without having any skills. I couldn't sell myself even to be a receptionist. As I teach and take on new and different roles, it strengthens my abilities in a very rounded way. I really love what I do, even on the days when it's stressful. The stress comes from having everybody needing something. Part of my job is to teach them that I can't always be everything, but that I care.

It's the most rewarding work I can imagine because every man who goes to class is making a choice. You lose a little time off your sentence, called 'good time.' I watch men who come in for good time end up staying because they're learning something and finding out they can do something positive. I've seen a lot of that this year because five, maybe even seven of them are eighteen- to twenty-one-year-olds. They are going to graduate [from high school].

I watched one man who had come very sporadically for a year just suddenly come on fire. I went in last Saturday, and he came up to me and said, 'What am I going to do when I graduate? Does that mean I can't come back anymore?' I just about cried. I said, 'No, you can come back as long as you want. I'll keep on preparing you to take college courses or vocational courses or whatever.' And that happens frequently.

I live my life trying to learn from the hard parts. It's not always easy. That's one thing my tutors have taught me: I have these little problems, and some big ones, but mostly little. They've been in jail and they've made big mistakes to get there. But now they're doing positive things and living in a positive way. One of them, I think, has never had as much trust in a person as he has in me. After four years of working with me, he gives back. I guess he never got back before this. 99

Index of Teachers

General Index

cultures. *See* teachers, and ethnicity

D

darkroom, 14
Darling-Hammond, Linda, *xi*
death row, 165
depression in student, 162
discipline in the classroom,
151–152
disciplines in biographical lead-
ins. *See also* schools
  arts or performing arts
    art, 20
    drama, 15, 92
    music, 34, 91, 140
    poetry, 112
    speech, 15, 40
    theater, 10
  computer literacy, 122
  computer science, 128
  computer/technology literacy,
    70–71
  education, 2
  English, 2, 10, 15, 32, 42, 58,
    61, 78, 81, 131, 156
  English as a Second Language,
    32, 37, 44, 46, 154
  foreign languages
    French, 8, 154
    Spanish, 18, 44, 63
  law enforcement, 58
  math, 8, 40, 52, 63, 64, 95, 128,
    135
  reading and language arts,
    15, 28, 40, 58, 63, 67, 106,
    137

science
  anatomy, 151
  biology, 87, 151
  earth science, 100
  endangered species, 87
  general, 37, 40, 63, 78, 95
  meteorology, 87
  oceanography, 87
  pediatrics, 110
  physics, 23
  physiology, 151
  psychology, 10, 73
social studies
  American history, 161
  history, 40, 125
  political science, 161
  Western civilization, 161
sports, 81, 116
discovery, learning as, 13
doctors, and their effects on others, 110–111
drugs or substance abuse, 18, 33,
  40–41
dyslexia, 28

E

earth as a classroom, 100–101
education, negotiating students'
  own, 137. *See also* disciplines
English as a Second Language,
  32, 37, 44, 46, 154
Eskimo culture, 148–150
ethics. *See* values

F

factory community, 10

farming community, 5, 15–16, 63, 65
fear of learning, 44–45
fit in, adolescents' desire to, 82
flannel board, 10
Foxfire training, 3

G

gang territory, 18
gifted children
  and behavior-disordered or learning disabled, 55, 106
  resource specialist for, 13
'good time,' in prisons, 165
guidance counselor, 128–130
guides, in Montessori classrooms, 46

H

Habitat for Humanity, 24
harmony, singing in, 141
hug, needing a, 157, 158
Hughes, Langston, 114
humor, sense of, 28

I

immigrants
  and Native Americans analogy, 126
  Polish, 44
impostor, feeling like an, 116
indoor river, 116
inmates as role models, 164
Inmates and Alternatives, 70, 71
inner-city kids, 152
Institute of American Indian Studies, 125

intelligence, nature of, *xi–xii*
Iñupiat, 149

J

jail, 33. *See also* prisons
jokes and riddles, 28
juggling, 85

K

kindness, remembered act of, 43
knowledge keepers, 127

L

learning disabilities, 28, 41, 56, 56–57, 67, 106, 109
linguist, Korean, 64
literature, getting students to appreciate, 59–60, 131, 132–133. *See also* disciplines
lottery system, 152

M

Marine Corps, 23
math. *See also* disciplines
  fear of, 95–96
  teaching to adults, 135–136
mentors, students as, 32, 37–38, 91
metaphors, writing in, 112
Mids for Kids, 24
migrating students, 156
multicultural issues, 35, 58. *See also* teachers, and ethnicity
music. *See also* disciplines
  and operas, 106–109
  as an outlet, 35–36

musicals
  putting on, 93–94
  with special-needs children,
    140–141

N

National Association for
    Humane and Bilingual
    Education (NAHABE),
    159
Native Americans, 103–105,
    125–127
nature walks, 13

O

opera as an educational medi-
    um, 106–109

P

parents
  abusive, 33, 55
  Apache, 104–105
  conferences with, 5, 48
  good relationships of teacher
    with, 116, 146
  learning from their children,
    63, 84
  of middle schoolers, 39, 47
  migrating, 156
  non–English speaking, 41
  reactions by, 25, 38, 47, 48,
    52
  students abandoned by, 157
  teachers acting as, 19, 60
  who taught, xi, 10, 65, 66, 110
Philadelphia Opera Company,
    106

picture books, used with all ages
    of children in crisis, 67–68
pilot, 23
pitch, singing on, 141–142
Plato, 30
play, as a teaching tool, 90
poetry, 126
  finding a reason to study,
    132–133
  'Sand Castle,' 30
  teaching to students, 112–115
police officer, 58
Polish students, 45
prayer, 105
pregnancy, teenage, 55
Presidential Awardee, 95
principal or administrator,
    being a, 92–93
prisons, 41, 71, 113, 164–166
puberty, 47, 78–79

Q

questions
  getting students to ask,
    161–162
  without answers, 155

R

racial issues. See teachers, and
    ethnicity
rape, 163
reading partners, 56
reservation
  Apache, 103–105
  Yankton Sioux, 125, 126–127
rural communities, 5, 15–16, 63,
    65

and long hours, 11
as mediators, 60
as mentors, 123
as role models, 8–9, 38–39, 89
as sounding boards, 47
who share with each other, 14
teaching
in alternative settings, 40–41,
113
and discipline in classroom,
151–152
fear of, 45
as gambling, 75
as a performance, 161
as a profession, *xi–xii*, 8, 9
and stress, 147
teams, and peer pressure, 81
technology in the classroom,
70–72
Technology-in-Learning, 122
time capsule, 5–6
tundra, 148

U

urban community, 152
Urban Systemic Initiative, 95

V

values, instilling in students, 16–
17, 22, 52, 60, 130, 137–139
vegetarian, 160
vet school, 65
vocation, versus occupation, 7

W

Web page, developing a, 122,
123

writing. *See also* disciplines
in adult-ed course, 135
creative, 112–115
in a journal, 47
with a partner, 56
poems, 112–115
reports in second grade, 84
for self-awareness, 137–138

XYZ

Yankton Sioux, 125
Youth Teaching Youth, 37